Higher Education and Global Challenges

Pallavi Maitra

Publishing House
4735/22, Prakash Deep Building,
Ansari Road, Daryaganj
New Delhi- 110002

Published by

SAURABH PUBLISHING HOUSE

Distributed by:

Lotus Press Publishers & Distributors

Unit No. 220, Second Floor, 4735/22, Prakash Deep Building,
Ansari Road, Darya Ganj, New Delhi-110002
Ph: 23280047, 32903912, 098118-38000
www.lotuspress.co.in

Saurabh Publishing is an imprint of
Lotus Press Publishers & Distributors

Higher Education For Global Challenges

ISBN 81-89005-02-2

Printed at: Afcons Enterprises, New Delhi

PREFACE

Higher Education and Global Challenges provides a forum for a comprehensive discussion of the nature of relationship between higher education and working life. Detailing three perspectives, namely those of society, higher education and the world of work, the book provides an in-depth coverage of issues and challenges facing students from the professional field, in the new millennium. Pedagogical perspective are greatly taken into account as the relationship between working life and higher education is critically examined and analysed, helping teachers modify their teaching ways to better equip their students with skills helping them to adapt better to a fast, evolving world.

Administration and management of higher education that hardly ever came under the preview of policy-makers and educationists, until recently, have also been effectively detailed. An entire chapter has been devoted to examining the challenges faced in terms of governance of higher education and a plethora of suggestions have been put forth to tackle these issues. Extending in-depth and thought-provoking analysis to all relevant but often ignored problems facing higher education, this book hopes to be insightful to researchers, undergraduate and postgraduate students of education and social sciences and university teachers interested in knowing how to better equip their students for future work.

Editor

CONTENTS

1

INTRODUCTON

Higher education is education provided by universities, vocational universities (community colleges, liberal arts colleges, and technical colleges, etc.) and other collegial institutions that award academic degrees, such as career colleges. Higher education, also referred to as tertiary education, is normally taken to include undergraduate and postgraduate education, as well as vocational education and training. Colleges and universities are the main institutions that provide tertiary education.

Higher education includes teaching, research and social services activities of universities, and within the realm of teaching, it includes both the undergraduate level (sometimes referred to as tertiary education) and the graduate (or postgraduate) level (sometimes referred to as graduate school). In most developed countries a high proportion of the population now enter higher education at some time in their lives. Higher education is therefore very important to national economies, both as a significant industry in its own right, and as a source of trained and educated personnel for the rest of the economy.

Higher education and training generally takes place in a university. Such education is based on theoretical expertise. Higher general education might be contrasted with higher vocational education, which concentrate on both practice and theory. A university is an institution of higher education and research, which grants degrees like Bachelor's degree, Master's degree and doctorates in a variety of subjects. However, most professional education is included within higher education, and many postgraduate qualifications are strongly vocationally or professionally oriented, for example in disciplines such as law and medicine.

EVOLUTION OF HIGHER EDUCATION

While it may not yet be possible to think of higher education as a global system, there is considerable convergence among the world's universities and higher education systems. The medieval European historical origin of most of the world's universities provides a common antecedent. The basic institutional model and structure of studies are similar worldwide.

Academic institutions have frequently been international in orientation—with common curricular elements and, in the medieval period, a common language of instruction—Latin. At the end of the 20th century, English has assumed a role as the primary international language of science and scholarship, including the Internet. Now, with more than one million students studying outside their borders, with countless scholars working internationally, and with new technologies such as the Internet fostering instantaneous communications, the international roots and the contemporary realities of the university are central.

Higher education systems have also been moving from elite to mass to universal access, as Martin Trow pointed out in the 1960s. In North America, much of Europe, and a number of East Asian countries, academic systems approach universal access, with close to half the relevant age group attending some kind of post-secondary institution and with access increasingly available for non-traditional students.

In some countries, however, access remains limited. In China and India, for example, despite dramatic expansion, under 5 percent of the age group attends post-secondary institutions. In some countries with relatively low per capita income, such as the Philippines, access is high, while in some wealthier nations, it remains a key point of challenge. Throughout Africa, access is limited to a tiny sector of the population. Access is an increasingly important issue everywhere, as populations demand it and as developing economies require skilled personnel. Demands for access come into conflict with another of the flashpoints of controversy of the present era—funding.

Higher education is an expensive undertaking, and there is much debate concerning how to fund expanding academic systems. Current approaches to higher education funding emphasise the need for "users" to pay for the cost of instruction, as policymakers increasingly view higher education as something that benefits the individual, rather than as a "public good" where the benefits accrue to society. This new thinking, combined with constrictions on public expenditures in many countries, have meant severe financial problems for academe. These difficulties come at a time when higher education systems are trying to provide expanded access.

Higher education's problems have been exacerbated in many of the poorer parts of the world by the idea, popular in the past several decades and stressed by the World Bank and other agencies, that basic education was most cost-effective—as a result, higher education was ignored by major lending and donor agencies. Now, higher education is back on the agenda of governments and multilateral agencies just as academe faces some of its most serious challenges.

Academic systems and institutions have tried to deal with these financial constraints in several ways. Loan programmes, the privatisation of some public institutions, and higher tuition are among the alternatives to direct government expenditure. In many parts of the world, including most of the major industrialised nations, conditions of study have deteriorated in response to financial constraints.

Enrolments have risen, but resources, including faculty, have not kept up with needs. Academic infrastructures, including libraries and laboratories, have been starved of funds. Less is spent on basic research. Conditions of study have deteriorated in many of the world's best-developed academic systems, including Germany and France. Students have taken to the streets in large numbers to protest declining budgets and poor conditions for the first time since the 1960s. There has also been a dramatic decline in academic conditions in sub-Saharan Africa and in some other developing areas.

While these trends vary to some extent from country to country, there is considerable convergence. Academic leaders worldwide worry about the same set of topics. Specific conditions vary from one country to another, and there are certainly major differences between the Netherlands and Mali. Yet, solutions from one country may be relevant, at least in terms of suggesting alternatives, elsewhere. For example, there is much interest in Australian ideas concerning a "graduate tax" – a repayment scheme based on postgraduate income. The United States, as the world's largest and in many respects leading academic system, experienced the challenges of universal access first, and American patterns of academic organisation are of considerable interest elsewhere.

We live in a period of rapid change in higher education, a period when we can learn much from the experience of others. In short, higher education has gone global but with a variety of accents. These global concerns or issues are actually not discrete topic areas. They are better understood as issue clusters.

HIGHER EDUCATION: CONTRIBUTION TO THE SOCIETY

In the last three centuries, the evolution of society has been amazing and has proceeded by many steps: from the agriculture society, to industrialisation, the post-industrial society, the information society, and, last, the knowledge society. The interacting context for people has changed dramatically. From the village, to the region, to the nation, to the continent, to the whole world, that characterises the knowledge society and the globalisation phenomena.

In the agriculture society, the larger part of the population lived and worked in the countryside or in small villages. Most of them could not read or write, they were taught by their relatives how to cope with the problems connected to cultivation and breeding, and learned on the job. Few people went to school and only very few reached a higher education level.

During the 17th and 18th centuries the development of science and technology produced the industrial revolution, with less and less people involved in the hard work of agriculture and more and more people leaving the countryside to live in big cities and to work in manufacturer industries. The industrial work asked for workers able to read and write and therefore primary education became soon compulsory in all the industrialised countries.

The French revolution produced the new concepts of national state and citizenship. The organisation of the society changed and new professions aroused to tackle the new needs of the population. Higher education institutions, and in particular universities, provided the professional skills and training, and educated the leaders for the new society. Universities became also the institutional places for producing knowledge through research activities.

In Europe up to the mid 20th century only a few percent of young people attended the university courses to reach a professional degree. After the Second World War the fast and widespread development of scientific knowledge and the impressive technological innovations produced a new displacement of people from the countryside to the cities and the new manufacturer industries asked for more and more educated workers. Therefore in Europe the compulsory period of studies of 5 years changed and shifted first to 8 years, then to 10-12 years. In the 60's and 70's the number of students attending the university courses was growing, reaching in some countries like USA the 50% of the age rank and in Europe about 20-30%.

Development of information and communication technology (ICT) and the great progress in transports – as high speed trains, cheap cars, larger and faster airplanes – improved a lot the mobility of people, goods, news, and ideas, giving rise to what we call today 'globalisation'. Information society in fact has been characterised by the spread of information that can bring to each person, every day, news about the whole world.

These developments affected deeply the geopolitical situation of the world and extended the complexity of the society. Today we talk of Asia, Europe, North America, etc. more than of single nations. Events like Olympic Games, world championships as well as regional wars like those in Kosovo or in Iraq are followed on television by billions of people all around the world. In the developed countries only a few percent of people are still involved in agriculture and only between 10-20% in industry. More and more are in fact engaged in the so-called 'third sector' in which are included all the services like national health services, teaching, research, transports, information and communication, sport and leisure activities, etc.

The incoming knowledge society puts on the table new problems and asks for new solutions. Land and natural resources have become less important; on the other hand human resources are crucial and strategic for the future of each country, thus making the investment in education and research the most fruitful. Through the media (television, newspapers, internet, etc) people share every day what happens in every part of the world and often the dramatic events prevail in this information. Therefore those who still live in undeveloped countries in poor conditions, becoming aware of their low level of living, ask for a better living environment and expect to reach the living standard of more evolved countries in a short time. At the same time people belonging to definite cultures and religions get in touch with people of different cultures and religions and the problem of how to manage a multicultural society arises.

The degree of development of one country is measured as the percent of growth in Gross National Product (GNP) and also as life expectation for the new generations. In fact the economical parameters are often the only ones taken into account. On the other hand the world resources limits do not allow the six billion people living today in our world to consume the average resources per person that is used in USA. Other problems as air pollution, drinking water availability, waste management, etc. can be faced and solved only at global level through global collaboration.

These are the reasons why the information society is becoming the knowledge society and the 'knowledge society' should evolve in the 'wisdom society' in order to face properly the new world situation. This asks for a deep change of mind and behaviour primarily in developed countries. To preserve the level of quality of life reached by developed countries it is necessary that other people improve faster their living conditions to reduce the gap between rich and poor countries. We can maintain our better conditions, but because of the limited resources in the world, we should at the same time reduce energy consumption, pollution, waste production, etc. In other words to measure the degree of comprehensive development for a country we have to introduce other non economic parameters such as the degree of education, the efficiency of the public health systems and of the public transports system, the impact on environment, etc.

Knowledge is an aware utilisation of information; wisdom means to behave following a shared knowledge in order to enhance the well being of everybody in the awareness that personal actions have a social consequence, and that today each part of the world is connected to the others. The knowledge is not only the scientific one which refers specifically to the natural world. It concerns also the artistic and humanistic world, and last but not least the spiritual and metaphysical world. In particular the spiritual and humanistic dimensions of the human being play a major role in giving meaning to the human life and contribute a lot to improve the quality of life.

If we want to contribute to realise a 'wisdom society' in which there is a wise use of knowledge it is necessary to develop in each person, in a well balanced way, the different dimensions of his/her being, i.e. the knowledge and economic dimensions together with the creative and spiritual dimensions. Each person should be aware of his/her responsibility to fully exploit his/her own potentialities and at the same time to act as a member of a society. In other words, everyone has to recover the consciousness of the social impact of his/her actions. If these are the real frames and the most likely perspectives of our society, it is very important to educate and train people for living and acting properly in this new, dynamic, and more and more complex society in the global context.

Role of Higher Education Institutions

Universities, colleges, higher education institutions, research centers have therefore to play a crucial role. As for information and knowledge society twelve years of school have been considered necessary, to shift from the knowledge to the wisdom society it is very important to extend as much as possible the higher education, both providing university courses and/or post baccalaureate courses to the largest possible number of young people and providing the opportunity to resume education many times during the life.

The wisdom society is a continuous learning society: every person has to act at the same time as learner and teacher in every context, therefore everybody must be taught how to learn and how to communicate; this should be not only the task of primary and secondary schools, but in particular the goal of higher education. In a knowledge society as well as in a wisdom society knowledge is expected to disseminate quickly and easily. This may create a tension between the needed knowledge certification and the needed knowledge diffusion. Many examples can be given: the knowledge on nuclear energy production and safety, the knowledge on the risks in the diffusion of GMO (Genetically Modified Organisms), or on the propagation of electromagnetic fields.

More and well educated people are necessary although this can not be sufficient. Therefore we have to extend higher education almost to everybody. Higher education should be supported mainly by public funds, because of the general needs that it has to fulfil and also to guarantee more independence to education and research. On the other hand we judge positively the payment of some fees by the students as thus they become more aware of the value of acquiring new knowledge and professional skills and therefore they feel compelled to a stronger engagement in their studies. Of course the principle that the students should contribute to the costs of their studies is a strong conflicting issue which needs to be reconciled with the possibility of access for everybody. Different solutions are possible with good results, provided they are coherent with the particular context.

The Bologna process is going on in Europe with different trends but to the same goal. A problem is still there: how to implement the teaching and learning for the cleverest people in order to exploit completely their potentiality? This is their own interest but also the interest of the whole society. In other words, how can we fulfil both the needs of mass education and the necessity to prepare good leaders? This can be done differentiating the institutions in mass and elite institutions or organising in the universities different support and opportunities for the best students, but both solutions can also be applied together.

Other problems have to be solved by higher education institutions. For example, what kind of competences should be developed by higher education, considering the fact that society is in fast evolution and that we have to provide young people with competences that must not become obsolete too fast? Higher education should be focused in developing primarily the 'core competences', i.e. the skills necessary to live in a complex, very interacting, and continuously changing society. Some of these 'core competences' are the capability of learning, listening, interacting, communicating, being active and proactive, solving problems, understanding other cultures and religions, etc. This implies for example to be able to manage the information and communication technologies, to speak and understand other languages, to be aware of one's own cultural identity.

Curricula and the teaching methods need to be changed and shaped for the new objectives. A greater flexibility in curricula is necessary, as well as more personalised interactions between students and teachers. A multidisciplinary approach to the problems should also be encouraged. Moreover 'education' must not remain a theoretical learning but the transfer of knowledge must be integrated with practical experience. Stages in working contexts are unavoidable means to educate young students to act, to be proactive and to learn how to evaluate themselves.

The new young generations come from families where the parents have been more engaged in realising themselves than in educating their children; they live in a continent where the traditional values have become weaker and people are opportunist and consumers. When they enter the University they seek the meaning of their life: they dream to meet the right person to create a real family, they hope to find a good job after graduation, and they also would like to contribute to change the society they know in a better one.

Universities have to take into account all these expectations and hopes, and provide their young students suitable opportunities and new means in order to facilitate their search of the meaning of life. Young students have to learn how to distinguish what is more important from what is trivial for their life. Universities should also present to the students models of behaviour, how to build up their own personality, and how to strengthen their own independence.

Role of Research and Innovation

A word which synthesises well the need of new approaches, new solutions, and new educational targets is 'innovation'. It is necessary to innovate in every field: technology, social sciences, politics, organisation, etc.: to innovate we have to develop in all these fields research activities, and we have to train more and more people to have an active role in research, in research transfer, and in exploitation of research results.

Intensive research universities are the main agents for basic research; they have the capability to be dynamic and effective engines for the development of knowledge society and economy, and a magnet for international talents. Europe must invest more money in basic research which is the source of creation of new knowledge and of most innovation in society. A clear and acceptable balance should be reached between the pursuit of knowledge for its own sake and the demand for basic research aimed at a tangible return to the economy and society at large.

The knowledge society not only needs excellence and top rate research but also depends on a larger number of highly educated people who, while not engaged in active research, have sufficient knowledge to make good use of the latest research results. To learn 'core competences' and to be trained in employability skills more and more students should have the opportunity to make stages in research groups and in other working environments, not only at doctoral level but also at graduate and undergraduate level.

As higher education and research are becoming more and more strategic activities for a new kind of development for our knowledge society the governments should proportionally increase their investments in research and higher education institutions. Universities seem to be the most suitable institutions for developing integrated activities of higher education, research, and innovation, and therefore they should be the main destinations of new public and private funds devoted to development. On the other hand, to optimise the exploitation of public and private funds given to universities it is necessary to enlarge the universities autonomy, to introduce both internal and external evaluation procedures, and to improve the social responsibility awareness of teachers, researchers and students.

The governments have the responsibility for the allocations of public funds and therefore they have to incentive and support the transfer of research results from laboratories to society. This can be done in different ways: certainly the more effective is through the mobility of people involved from labs to industry and society and vice versa. Again this can be enhanced if bureaucratic obstacles are removed: the mobility of researchers should not have negative consequences on their careers and in particular on social benefits as health care and future amounts of pensions. This asks for a new legislation at European level that overcomes the single state present rules.

Due to the limitation of public funds for research, also in case they would be increased as everybody asks for, the problem of setting the priorities is ever present. The public funds for research should be divided in three categories: the first should be devoted to fertilise the free research, and allocated according to the quality of researchers. The second should be devoted to basic research and allocated to the large fields evaluated more important for society growth. The third should be devoted to applied and finalised research, taking into account the actual needs of society.

In a democratic country the division of research funds between these categories must be responsibility of the government and the parliament. Then the allocation of each part should be decided by the scientific and academic community for the first two categories; for the third, the academic and scientific community can decide jointly with people coming from industry and other productive realities.

The 'wisdom society' should be characterised by a greater institutions autonomy, more personal responsibility, and fewer rules: the governments must facilitate and fund more research in humanities and social sciences to educate people to manage properly at personal and global level science achievements and technological development, in order to foster the personal and social growth. To improve personal responsibility based on shared strong values it is better to trust the role of faiths and religions as traditional regulators of good personal behaviour than to try to control the growing complexity of the society and the personal actions only by augmenting the number of laws and rules approved by parliaments or governments.

INTERNATIONAL TRENDS IN HIGHER EDUCATION

In the era of knowledge-driven economy and learning societies, both formal and informal education is playing an increasingly vital role in promoting economic solidarity, social cohesion, individual growth, sustainable development, and a culture of peace and world citizenship. Whereas our views about the way we live, learn, work, and 'think about work' have changed, the acquisition of knowledge and skills provided by a traditional formal educational setup do not correspond. Therefore, a new paradigm must evolve that is developmental, human-centered, environmentally sound, and all-inclusive, so as to prepare learners to be contributors to knowledge and not just mere recipients of knowledge. It has opened up new challenges and opportunities for higher education institutions – whether public, private, or hybrid. Just a few years ago, we could not have imagined a university without classrooms, or a library without books. Nor could we imagine a university existing 10,000 miles away from its students. Nor could we imagine technocrats rather than faculty and academic staff managing sensitive information and knowledge 'online'. Yet all of this is true today. The University of Phoenix, for example, one of the most dynamic amongst the distance learning universities, has an enrolment of over 200,000 students across the world.

Science and technology parks have lately emerged in the education sector, based upon public-private partnerships for research activities. We find such science parks in Taipei, Japan, and Singapore. In Taipei, for instance, there is a science-based industrial park at Hsinchu. It has been built near the major universities with both government and private support, and it has attracted the attention of many hi-tech firms in China and other parts of the world.

Additionally, some university-owned firms, partly funded by the private sector, are producing certain products for the educational market. A number of universities are entering into contracts with private publishers. Similarly, a large number of private enterprises are entering into agreements with various universities to meet their technological and other requirements or to help them with the distribution of their knowledge-based products. There are abundant examples of private booksellers, food services, and providers of other services, academic and non-academic alike.

Given the increasingly corporate culture in higher education, it is not surprising that 'education' has been included as a 'service' or a 'commodity' under the General Agreement on Trade and Tariffs (GATT) and World Trade Organisation (WTO). Though UNESCO has been striving hard towards protecting and strengthening higher education as a common good at the global level by promoting pluralism and diversity, on the one hand, and equitable access, capacity building, and sharing of knowledge, on the other, the GATS and WTO are striving equally hard towards reducing the barriers to 'trade' in higher education. No wonder, then, that we find the academic institutions and business enterprises of the North actively selling educational programmes to middle-income and emerging economies in the South.

The former have made collaborative arrangements with overseas institutions or offshore campuses via distance or online education. They are able to use new technologies and international collaboration effectively and rapidly for the education of approximately 84 million students attending about 2000 universities and colleges worldwide. These institutions operate in a largely unregulated environment, although organisations like GATE (The Global Alliance for Transnational Education) have recently come to the forefront with the aim of fostering and maintaining quality in cross-border higher education enterprises.

The concept of private higher education is not new. In Asia, private institutions have always been a central part of higher education. Private higher education has been playing a major role in Japan, South Korea, Taiwan, Taipei, Indonesia, and the Philippines. In these countries, up to 80 percent of students attend private institutions. Private higher education is reported to be rapidly growing in China, Vietnam, Cambodia, and other central Asian republics as well. Generally, private post-secondary institutions are found to be at the lower end in terms of prestige, though there are some high quality private universities, such as Waseda and Keio in Japan, De La Salle and the Ateneo de Manila in the Philippines, Yonsei in South Korea, and Santa Dharma in Indonesia. These universities are among the oldest in their respective countries and share a reputation of training the elite class.

Another category of new private institutions comprises those specialising in fields such as management, technology, or education, with the sole aim of offering high quality academic degrees having market acceptability. The Asian Institute of Technology in the Philippines and the National Institute of Information Technology in India fall in this category. Besides private universities and colleges serving the mass higher education market on a massive scale, there are some non-selective institutions run by individuals or families. There are also some institutions sponsored by private, non-profit religious groups or ethnic organisations.

Many Asian countries already have considerable experience in managing private higher education institutions on a large scale, whereas other countries have picked this up during the last 25 to 30 years. Whereas we find a long tradition of private higher education in Asia, we find dramatic changes in terms of the public-private mix in Eastern Europe in the last few years. There are 91 private business schools in Poland, 29 in the Czech Republic, 21 in Armenia, 18 in Romania, and 4 in Bulgaria. In the Cote d'Ivoire, professional training is exclusively in the private domain, and in Gambia 44% of skill-based education and training is privately provided. About 75% of tertiary education in India is supposed to be under private management. Whereas most of the private colleges are affiliated with the open schools or public universities, we also find examples of new private universities being set up under the Private Universities

Acts passed by some of the newly emergent states in India such as Chattisgarh or Uttaranchal.

China has more than 1200 private higher education institutions today, though not all of them enjoy official government authorisation. By the end of 2002, only 4 private colleges had been authorised to award the bachelor's degree and 129 were authorised to grant degrees below the level of the bachelor's. The private sector accounts for 10% of the total enrollment in post-secondary education in China. Whereas the public-private educational institutions in Shanghai and Beijing enjoy reasonably good reputations, the schools in Shenyang are not doing so well. These Minban Gongzhu (owned and supported by the government through property and infrastructure) are seen as breeding corruption, sacrificing quality for the sake of profit, and putting unnecessary pressures on students and their families.

The notion of private ownership is different in China from that prevailing in the western world. Minban or Sili (private institutions) remain only partly owned by the government and administered by independent parties. On 28 December 2002, China promulgated its first national legislation on private education. The law aimed at facilitating private growth and initiated a longer process to accredit, merge, dismantle, or change institutions at higher level. China's initial recognition of private education under the 1982 constitution was quite vague and timely action was required to provide legitimacy to the private institutions engaged in higher education.

These institutions are now playing an important role in filling the gap between demand and supply, on the one hand, and stemming the brain drain by providing job opportunities to many local Chinese, on the other. Unlike China, private higher education in post-communist

Russia is only a decade old and public involvement in the creation of private higher education institutions has been substantial. Russian private higher education institutions are generally referred to as 'non-state' institutions to demarcate them from both the government and private institutions. Though these institutions are not funded by the central government, they rely considerably on support and resources from other state-run organisations and agencies. Often their connection to government bodies is much closer than is openly declared.

There are more than 500 private institutions that account for roughly 10 percent of enrollment in higher education, mostly under market-related programmes such as economics, law, psychology, sociology, social work, business administration, and other such fields that do not require much investment, equipment, or research facilities. Similarly, in Vietnam, about 12% of the students attend "nonpublic institutions". There the first non-public institution, known as the Thang Long University, was established in 1989 on an experimental basis. By 2002-3, Vietnam had 23 non-public post-secondary institutions. Out of these, 16 were people-founded universities, 2 were people-founded colleges, 1 was a semi-public university, and 4 were semi-public colleges. People founded institutions are owned and managed by the NGOs or private associations, whereas the semi-public institutions are owned and operated by the public authorities with some private support. In future, private individuals may also own and operate nonpublic higher educational institutions along with some foreign-owned institutions.

In Malaysia there has been rapid growth of private higher education. There are 691 private colleges and universities and 4 foreign university campuses. Malaysia is one of a few countries that had long ago allowed private higher education, without granting it full status. Recently the government has put restrictions on funding study abroad programmes. Instead it is striving hard to attract foreign students from neighboring countries by making Malaysia an educational hub. In fact, between 1997 and 2000, foreign enrollment grew by 60% in Malaysia. Malaysia relies on the private sector both to meet the excessive demand for higher education and technical skills, and to generate revenues from abroad.

The private sector is making inroads into higher education in the Middle East, as well. For instance, in Afghanistan, along with political and economic changes, we find equivalent changes in the education sector. The Afghan government is actively planning for the first private university, the American University of Afghanistan. This university is to be American style, with English as the medium of instruction and mainly American professors as faculty.

In Saudi Arabia, the government has given permission to private organisations to set up 2 new universities and 36 colleges as part of its privatisation policy. The colleges are to be spread over the 9 cities and are to be in addition to 6 already existing private colleges with licenses from the Ministry of Higher Education.

In Latin America, the oldest universities are private institutions set up by the Catholic Church. But now the trend is in favour of for-profit private universities. For instance, the University of the Americas, owned by Sylvan Learning System, is making big profits despite deriving criticism from Chile's academia for lower quality and higher fees. This private university, however, prides itself on offering access and international ties. Surprisingly, the private sector in Chile is allowed to function *de facto*, even if it is not granted *de jure* status. But in Argentina, private higher education institutions have been allowed full license for a provisional period of time. The private sector has now captured a fifth of university enrollments and a fourth of total higher education enrollments there.

There is a long tradition of private career colleges in Canada. Today even the public universities are working very hard to pursue private links. Their focus is on internationalisation as a proactive response to the worldwide circulation of ideas, technology, capital, and people. There is a wide range of private post-secondary institutions working in Canada, offering programmes in areas such as aviation, business, computer training, hospitality, tourism, and English as second language, among others. While these institutions are required to register with the provincial government, they are not accredited directly by the government. Rather, the institutions may be encouraged to apply for accreditation by the Private Post-secondary Education Commissions in their respective provinces. Canada is the first country to have passed the Private Post-secondary Education Act in 1996 in order to protect the interests of students and their families as consumers.

In the United States, some of the private institutions are able to focus on 'quality education' and 'narrow purpose'. The rationale behind private post-secondary education seems to be high quality, high costs, and high prestige, on the one hand, and cultural distinctiveness and additional services, on the other. No wonder the private for-profit post-secondary institutions are doing well, whereas traditional public universities and colleges are often struggling financially.

In the case of private post-secondary education, the market and short-term considerations have an edge over academics and long-term goals. Private equity funds are investing hugely in the US for profit higher education market in the wake of increasing job market and political acceptance of these institutions. Traditional colleges and universities are also investing in private for-profit education themselves.

Whereas private higher education is growing worldwide in response to a number of factors and with a variety of goals—meeting the demand for advanced levels of knowledge and technological skills that exceeds the supply; providing more choices or differentiated products to meet the specific demands of the students as consumers and clients; more feasibly implementing variable fee structures on the basis of ability to pay; adopting practices from business management to increase accountability and economic efficiency; shouldering some governmental burdens; rectifying inegalitarian, over-, or mis-use of public provision of higher education; making the government focus on its prime duty towards literacy and basic education; saving public subsidies for public goods; generating revenues and making innovations through experimentation—there can be significant variations at the socio-cultural and national levels.

Most of the Western European countries are still dominated by public universities, while private higher education is becoming more successful in Eastern Europe. In the United Kingdom and many other countries, the distinction between public and private colleges is getting blurrier by the day. One of the reasons is the competition from the new private post-secondary institutions that are more affordable and market-oriented. Another is the change in public policies regarding private initiative in post-secondary education. We also find some new institutions financed by a mixture of public and private resources. Governments are no longer indifferent or hostile to the private sector in most countries.

But there is no dearth of examples of the post-secondary private institutions unable to survive in the wake of harsh competition and demand for quality education. For instance, many institutions were forced to close down in Japan. Poor economic performance, falling birth rates, and a decade-old recession were reported to be the prime factors responsible for their closure. Some of the private higher education institutions could not survive as, in Japan, faculty salaries were accounting for 60-70% of operating costs.

In Mexico, where the number of private universities rose from 67 in 1975 to 1368 in 2003, the government has had to close 88 private universities over the past two years for failing to comply with basic educational standards. In the same vein, the Ugandan government has had to clamp down on private tertiary institutions operating illegally. The National Council for Higher education in Uganda published a list of 13 private degree-awarding authorities that it licensed and warned against enrolling in non-authorised institutions. Uganda is representative of most African countries, where we find a sharp rise in private higher education. Most of it has occurred as "unregulated surprise" and "unanticipated development". In most of these cases, the governments are engaged in more clearly defining roles in private higher education, regulating these institutions, and guarding the interests of the students as clients against low quality suppliers in open markets.

Kenya, on the other hand, provides another example where the number of students seeking private higher education is declining. In Kenya, private higher education has a longer history than in most other states in Africa, but their share in student enrollment is declining as a result of the adoption of the Module II programme by the public universities. Here the private universities are also facing challenges from entrepreneurial foreign universities from South Africa, the UK, and Australia.

In most African countries, the assessment and accreditation bodies have been set up by national or provincial governments to regulate quality, curricula, fee structures, faculty competence, accessibility, etc. A large number of private higher education institutions end up filling the gap between supply and demand or performing traditional socio-economic functions. Most of them remain public as far as their missions are concerned. Private institutions worldwide are generally criticised for their privateness, their lack of quality or accessibility, or their contribution to the commercialisation or commodification of higher education.

It is not generally recognised, however, that it is always the 'private' that dominates both the public and the private. Neither privatisation nor nationalisation could have occurred without the prior consensus or nexus between business and politics. Moreover, the private sector can cater to diversified needs on a smaller or more select basis more easily than can the public sector. In fact, the private sector can also be given credit for the expansion of higher education in most countries in the last three decades. It can provide quality education to the elite, vocational education to the needy, and low quality education to those who neither merit nor can afford a better education. It can also provide education to those who are already employed, through distance or online education on an "anytime, anywhere" basis.

HIGHER EDUCATION : GLOBAL CONCERNS

In the last decade, higher education has emerged as a key sector in the social and economic transition taking place in countries around the world. The concerns of the public and of politicians have focused on higher education in a number of ways. The world society suffered a critical loss of intellectual resources due to national disintegration, political purges, brain drain, and market restructuring. Higher education has provided an important recruitment base for the newly emerging political arena. Faculty and students have become part of a new breed of public personalities, which allows representatives of the sector to gain more influence and thus retain or even enhance their political privileges.

Higher education is increasingly seen as a leading force to help transitional societies catch up with wealthy nations. In many countries, higher education as a sector has experienced deprivation and crisis, given the problems of feasibility and sustainability. In countries that have gone through civil conflicts and violent confrontations, the resulting physical destruction has made costly rehabilitation programmes necessary that are hardly feasible. In countries that have experienced economic and financial deterioration, the inadequately maintained infrastructure and devalued salaries have left higher education in turmoil, as sustaining quality or even basic services does not seem possible.

Higher education has profoundly changed in the past two decades, and those involved in the academic enterprise have yet to grapple with the implications of these changes. Academic institutions and systems have faced pressures of increasing numbers of students and demographic changes, demands for accountability, reconsideration of the social and economic role of higher education, implications of the end of the Cold War, and the impact of new technologies, among others. While academic systems function in a national environment, the challenges play themselves out on a global scale.

We identify several themes that seem to be central to current developments in higher education worldwide. These themes deserve elaboration and analysis. They affect countries and regions differently, although we believe that all are relevant internationally, and that a discussion of implications can lead to understanding that will be useful for both comparative and national analysis.

– Education and work are activities that should feed one another. The links and transition points from initial education to the work force are weakly articulated. This is true in the developed world as well as in the developing world. Educators and business leaders rarely discuss, let alone agree upon, a set of skills and orientations that are prerequisites for successful employment. The formal structures by which education systems prepare students for tomorrow are similarly weakly developed. Models developed in Germany, through the linking of post-secondary education and apprenticeship arrangements, or community college system are currently being explored in several areas. Professional education often links well to employment in many countries, but education in the arts and sciences is less well articulated. It is not clear how close an articulation is possible, but the issues are worthy of further consideration.

– While the initial transition from school to work may be poorly articulated, the demand for education throughout the life cycle is becoming apparent. Fed by rapid changes in technology and the creation of employment categories that did not exist 10 years ago, workers and employers must continually attend to the educational dimension. As the nature of work has evolved, so have the needs of those in the workforce to continually upgrade their capacities. This has led to the development of a variety of educational forms beyond the bachelor's degree. In Germany, recent changes in the degree structure have led to the modularisation of graduate degrees. In the United States, certificate programmes and short-term courses of study are being rapidly developed. By one recent estimate corporations in the United States alone will spend

$15 billion over current expenditures by 2005 just to maintain current employee training levels. Others estimate that worldwide expenditures on training amount to many billions of dollars annually to ensure that their workforce has the skills necessary to compete in an ever-competitive and high-velocity business environment. In many countries, especially in the developing world, graduate education is coming into its own as the need for advanced skills and for continuing education becomes increasingly clear.

– It has become a point of banality to remark on the changes that technological developments have wrought. Indeed, many of the dislocations in school-to-work transition and the press for lifelong education are partially the result of these developments. More directly, however, technology has made possible a revolution in distance education that has important implications for the accreditation of educational institutions and assurance of quality in such circumstances. Technology is also beginning to have an impact on teaching and learning in traditional universities. It is also a truism that this technology is expensive, subject to rapid obsolescence, and requires high initial investment simply to get into the game. For many developing countries, cost is at present prohibitive, and it is precisely these areas where technology can provide the greatest short-term improvement. Technology is also central to the communication, storage, and retrieval of knowledge. The traditional library is being revolutionised by web-based information systems, as are the management systems of many universities.

– As the market for individuals with transnational competencies has grown, so have opportunities for individuals with marketable skills in other countries. Currently, the transfer of talent has been from developing countries such as India and China to the developed world. In the United States, the stay rates for advanced students in the engineering disciplines and the sciences can be higher than 75 percent for students from particular countries. From the perspective of national education authorities, these students may represent a considerable hemorrhaging of talent that has been developed by the students' countries of origin. If nations are to develop, a means must be found by which talent can flourish in the soils that originally nurtured it. Related issues of internationalising the curriculum and providing a global consciousness to students, including instruction in foreign language, and ensuring that the academic profession is linked internationally are central to any discussion of the internationalisation of higher education.

– Although seldom discussed, one of the areas of greatest expansion worldwide has been graduate education—the post-baccalaureate training for the professions as well as for science, technology, and teaching. Graduate education offers great opportunities for international links and cooperation. Countries can take advantage of graduate training capacities elsewhere, and the new technologies can provide key links. Highly specialised and advanced-level teaching and research deserve careful analysis.

– The privatisation of higher education is a worldwide phenomenon of considerable importance. In Latin America and some parts of Asia, the fastest-growing parts of the academic system are private institutions. In Central and Eastern Europe, private initiative is also of considerable importance. Public universities are in some places being "privatised" in the sense that they are increasingly responsible for raising their own funds. They are asked to relate more directly to society. Students are increasingly seen as "customers." The expansion of the private sector brings up issues of quality control and accreditation since in many parts of the world there are few controls as yet on private-sector expansion. Access is also a central issue. As some developing areas, such as sub-Saharan Africa, will soon be experiencing the growth of private institutions, understanding in a comparative context the problems and possibilities of private higher education is an urgent need.

- The academic profession is in crisis almost everywhere. There is a rapid growth of part-time faculty members in many countries, and traditional tenure systems are under attack. The professoriate is being asked to do more with less, and student-teacher ratios, academic salaries, and morale have all deteriorated. The professoriate is being asked to adjust to new circumstances but is given few resources to assist in the transition. Without a committed academic profession, the university cannot be an effective institution.
- Access and equity remain central factors, but in the current policy context are sometimes ignored. While academic systems worldwide have expanded dramatically, there are problems of access and equity in many parts of the world. Gender, ethnicity, and social class remain serious issues. In many developing countries, higher education remains mainly an urban phenomenon, and one

that is reserved largely for wealthier segments of society. Although women have made significant advances, access for women remains a serious problem in many parts of the world.

- Accountability is a contemporary watchword in higher education. Demands by funding sources, mainly government, to measure academic productivity, control funding allocations, etc. is increasingly a central part of the debate on higher education. Governance systems are being strained, sometimes to the breaking point. To meet the demands for accountability, universities are becoming "managerialised," with professional administrators gaining increasing control. The traditional power of the professoriate is being weakened.
- Expansion brings with it increased differentiation and the emergence of academic systems. New kinds of academic institutions emerge, and existing universities serve larger and more diverse groups. In order to make sense of this differentiation, academic systems are organised to provide coordination and the appropriate management of resources.

These are some of the key topics that affect contemporary post-secondary education worldwide. While this is by no means a complete list, it provides the basis for discussion and cooperation. International and comparative analysis can help to yield insights on how to deal with these topics in individual countries.

Institutions of higher education have historically played an important role in serving the globe. Today, like many other elements of our society, higher education is under stress, with rising tuitions, growing barriers for low income and minority students, and increasing privatisation of public institutions. Conservative anti-tax/anti-government ideology has taken its toll as states struggle to fund their public universities and community colleges. At the same time, the open academic environment and academic freedom have become increasingly vulnerable to commercial pressures, attacks on science, government security measures and occasional right-wing political monitoring of individual faculty members. Institutions of higher education remain remarkable in their diversity, intellectual strength and commitment to openness. These are opportunities that should be accessible to all citizebs, not a privileged elite. The democratising of access to universities will only strengthen and improve education. Harnessing the intellectual energy of universities for enlightened public ends will strengthen the nations.

2

IMPACT OF GLOBALISATION ON HIGHER EDUCATION

Globalisation is a newly emerging phenomenon. It has been defined as a set of processes by which the world is rapidly being integrated into one economic space via increased international trade, the internationalisation of production and financial markets; the internationalisation of a commodity culture promoted by an increasingly networked global telecommunication system. It transcends socio-economic and political barriers that the countries of the world are prone to build around themselves. It is not only a process integrating just economy, but culture, technology and governance. It is giving rise to new markets, foreign exchange and capital markets linked globally, new tools, internet links, cellular phones, media network, new actors; the World Trade Organisation with authority over national governments, the multi-national cooperation with more economic power than many states, new rules, multi-national agreements and intellectual property, multi-lateral agreements on trade.

Globalisation is expected to have a positive influence on the volume, quality and spread of knowledge through increased interaction among the various states. 'In a globalised world, as technology becomes its main motor, knowledge assumes a powerful role in production, making its possession essential for nations, if they are successfully to pursue economic growth and competitiveness. Education, being the most potent instrument of creation, assimilation and transmission of knowledge, assumes a central role in the process.

In a market oriented competitive world, unleashed by the forces of globalisation, education has to assume a somewhat different role. It cannot afford to be conventional, rigid and impervious to change. It has to keep abreast of the latest developments in various fields and be capable of creating, absorbing and transacting neo-technology and information systems that are sweeping across the countries of the world. There has also to be a paradigm shift in the contents of education with substantial emphasis on the productivity aspect of the curriculum. It would also call for adequate emphasis on research and development. It is, however, necessary to guard against being swept off our feet by the new 'cult of technology', and consequently, 'the diminution of respect for spiritual and cultural values'. An unfettered and ruthless pursuit of economic goals, without regard to considerations of moral and social values is bound to be disastrous for the people, particularly in developing countries.

In spite of the cataclysmic changes brought about in most countries, it would be wrong to consider globalisation as a panacea for all economic and social ills. The accelerated process of liberalisation and globalisation in the world has increased the opportunities for growth and development, but it has also added new complexities and risks in the management of global interdependence". Some of the complexities identified at the international level are:

— Globalisation is forging greater interdependence, yet the World seems more fragmented - between the rich and the poor, between the powerful and the powerless.

- Economically, politically and technologically, the world has never seemed more free - or more unjust.
- If the present global progress continues at such a snails' pace, it will take more than 130 years to rid the World of hunger.
- Globalisation is a "tricky term for some, it connotes free flow of ideas, capital, people and goods around the world. For others, it implies the hegemony of the capitalist system, the domination of rich nations and corporations and the loss of national identity.

It would thus appear that globalisation is not an unmixed blessing. It may promote "growth through increased technology and knowledge transfers in developing countries but it could also be sometime a source of instability.

The changes to which higher education all over the globe increasingly is exposed, are complex and varied, even contradictory, and the comprehensive concept of globalisation are far from clear and well defined. Nevertheless, the concept of globalisation indicates that the various changes are somehow interrelated and creating new forms of interdependencies between actors, institutions and states. For the sake of this chapter , we stress the following tendencies within the overall force of globalisation:

- *the rise of the 'network' society*, driven by technological innovation and the increasing strategic importance of information, and symbolised by the expansion of the Internet;
- *the restructuring of the economic world system*, with the transformation to a post-industrial knowledge

economy in the core, the emergence of newly industrialised nations, and the growth of new forms of dependency in the developing world; the rapid integration of the world economy with increasingly liberalised trade and commerce, resulting in new opportunities but also in relocation of production;

- *the political reshaping of the post-Cold World War order*, with strategic shifts in power balances and the emergence of new regions challenging the hegemony of the 20th Century superpowers, but also with increasing global insecurity and an endless list of regional and local conflicts;
- *the growing real but also virtual mobility* of people, capital and knowledge, possible because of new transport facilities, the development of the Internet and an increasingly integrated world community, but also provoked by the will among the hopeless to escape poverty, new mass migrations and refugees escaping war and insecurity;
- *the erosion of the nation-state* and its capacity to master the economic and political transformations, together with the weakness of the international community and its organisations, widening the gap between economic activity and socio-political regulation, and leading to unbound global capitalism but also to new international forms of crime;
- *the very complex cultural developments*, with on the one hand aspects of homogenisation such as an increasing cultural exchange and multicultural reality, but also the worldwide hegemony of the English language and the spread of commercial culture, and on the other hand elements of cultural differentiation and segregation such as funda-

mentalisms of various kinds (including new nationalisms), regressive tendencies, intolerance and a general feeling of loss of identity.

These forces and tendencies are not the only ones which define the social environment in which higher education has to operate at the start of the 21st century; reference has to be made as well to the demographic challenges, the spread of aids, endemic poverty or religious conflicts, just to name a few. Globalisation also means that institutions and even states no longer can give their own answers to all these challenges, but that they also have become interdependent in their policy-making processes.

GLOBALISATION AND ISSUES IN HIGHER EDUCATION

Education, as a service industry, is part of globalisation process under the umbrella of General Agreement on Trade in Services (GATS). There is, however, distinct possibility that this might force countries with quite different academic needs and resources to conform to structures inevitably designed to service the interest of the most powerful academic systems and corporate educational providers breeding inequality and dependence. Globalisation can lead to unregulated and poor quality higher education, with the world wide marketing of fraudulent degrees or other so-called higher education credentials. While these are obvious problems, globalisation can also have advantages, particularly for India, which has a large educational system and infrastructure and diverse human capabilities.

Given the array of theoretical and epistemological perspective presented in the general social science literature on 'globalisation', it is difficult to assess not only the nature and dimensions of globalisation, but also what it might mean to the field of education. Very few educational researchers or theorists have attempted to make connections between the economic, political and cultural dimensions of globalisation and the policies and practices of education.

It appears as though the phenomenon of globalisation will mean many different things for education. Most certainly, in the near future, "it will mean a more competitive and deregulated educational system modelled after free market but with more pressure on it to assure that the next generation of workers are prepared for some amorphous 'job market of 21st century'. It will also mean... "that educational system will increasingly provide the sites of struggle over the meaning and power of national identity and a national culture. And finally, schools will no doubt also be the sites of various counter-hegemonic movements and pedagogies".

Globalisation, though a recent phenomenon, is a reality, which cannot be wished away. It is, however, difficult to measure its long-term effect on the course of socio-economic development in various countries. In fact, because of the large disparities in the economic position of the countries inhabiting the globe, it would be imprudent to arrive at any standardised formula of assessing the effects. Each country is an entity in itself and requires to be studied differently. It is however necessary to stress that a thoughtless and unimaginative entry into the globalised market would not be in the best interests of the countries, particularly those, which are striving to grapple with the problems of slow economic and social development.

The impact of the various trends and challenges related to globalisation on higher education institutions and policies is profound, but also diverse, depending on the specific location in the global arena. There is a danger of generalisation and oversimplification when dealing with globalisation; diversity has to be recognised but also to a certain extent promoted. Nevertheless, an attempt can be made to define some general tendencies in higher education that in one way or another relate to globalisation:

Globalisation and Knowledge Society

Globalisation and the transition to a knowledge society seem to create new and tremendously important demands and exigencies towards universities as knowledge-centres. Scientific research and development of technologies are crucial activities in a knowledge and information driven society and will become even more important in the future. Not only in the core countries of the developed world, but increasingly also in other parts of the globe will research and development activities become the motor of economic growth and social development. Because there is a move away from the traditional scientific research paradigm and towards more 'Mode 2' oriented research, and because of the fact that also outside the fields of natural sciences research becomes strategically important for corporations and governments, the role and importance of science and technology will continue to grow. Since long, scientific research is intrinsically internationally oriented, but the internationalisation of research has accelerated strongly during the last years.

International communication (publishing, conferences, electronic networking) within the scientific community and quality norms for scientific personnel benchmarked to international standards have to be developed by universities that aspire the quality label of research universities. As a side effect of the globalisation of research and development, the academic profession itself becomes more mobile and an highly competitive international market of researchers is emerging, with organised migration of researchers and brain drain as one of the consequences. The new role of universities as 'knowledge centres' stretches out to other functions than science and research however. Universities are called upon to take up responsibilities in society and culture at large, to act as mediators in conflicts, to deepen democracy, to dynamise cultures, to function as centres for critical debate and ethical conscience. The high demands placed upon universities worldwide create tensions in institutions, and at the same time stimulate other organisations to engage also in those kinds of activities, sometimes with the idea in mind that traditional universities will not be able to meet those new demands.

Increasing Demand for Higher Education

Many observers expect an increase in the demand for higher education worldwide. In the developed world the knowledge society will ask for even more highly qualified knowledge workers. Economic development, modernisation and demographic pressure will fuel the demand for higher education also in other parts of the world, only limited by the inability of the poor to finance the cost of higher learning. Local institutions nor governments will have enough resources to deal with this massification of demand in many countries, leaving an unmet demand in the upper and middle classes of many countries in the ex-Soviet Union and the southern hemisphere to international and virtual providers.

The demand for higher education will not only grow quantitatively but will also become more diverse. Despite some decline in their value as credentials on the labour market in the developed world, traditional qualifications (degrees and diplomas) will remain the most important product of higher education institutions, but they will be supplemented by specialised programmes, vocational and competency-oriented training and modular courses adapted to a new lifelong learning demand, even if higher education institutions are not the main providers in these fields in many countries. In other parts of the world however, credentialism still is on the rise, sometimes leading to a kind of 'paper chase', fuelled by the (sometimes overrated) expectation that degrees and diplomas are the gateway to economic prosperity and social security by promising a job in the public sector.

New communication technologies and the Internet provide new opportunities for a more flexible delivery of higher education, thereby creating a new demand in some countries and meeting demand in others where traditional institutions are incapable to do so. All together, these developments underpin the assertion that higher education will become one of the booming markets in the years to come. This expansion and massification will not be matched by a proportional rise in public expenditure, leading to an increase in private and commercial provision and creating huge problems of access and equity.

Regulatory Issues

Internationalisation and globalisation lead to an erosion of the national regulatory and policy frameworks in which universities are embedded. Most modern higher education institutions are product of national developments and policies and are fully integrated in national educational systems. In an increasingly international environment—marked by a globalised and liberalised marketplace, globalising professions, mobility of skilled labour, an international arena of scientific research and academic personnel, and international competition between universities and between universities and other institutions and companies –, the national character of policy frameworks creates more and more tensions. Institutions already acknowledge this and are developing partnerships, consortia and networks to strengthen their position in the global arena.

Mobility programmes, such as ERASMUS/ SOCRATES or UMAP, and schemes such as the European credit transfer system have tried to stimulate internationalisation in higher education with full respect to the various national policy frameworks. Globalisation challenges this more or less voluntaristic policy and asks for more thorough international harmonisation of policy frameworks, higher education structures, degree systems and even curricula.

The process started with the Bologna-Declaration in Europe is a clear example of this, but in the context of free-trade agreements, like for example NAFTA or MERCOSUR, similar tendencies of international harmonisation of higher education systems exist also in other parts of the world. In the longer run this eventually will lead to the generalisation of the bachelor/master-degree structure, the hegemony of English as the lingua franca in higher education and scientific research, the development of compatible credit transfer and accumulation systems to recognise, transport and validate teaching and learning experiences, the international recognition of degrees and diplomas, a negotiated consensus on core knowledge and competencies and their place in curricula, especially in specific professional fields, etc.

Like in other social fields, globalisation will create resistance and counter tendencies in the field of higher education, asking for the recognition of the importance of the national language, the specific degree architecture, the cultural embeddedness of curricula, etc. Such tendencies are not always to be seen as retrograde or counter-productive to globalisation. Globalisation in higher education does not necessarily imply international standardisation and uniformity, but asks for policies balancing the global and the local.

To a large extent resistance to globalisation in higher education is also motivated by a rejection of the marketisation perceived to be inherent in globalisation and a defence of a 'public good' approach to higher education. However, many make the error to identify a 'public good' perspective towards higher education with an exclusively national policy framework. An international regulatory framework is needed to transcend the eroded national policy contexts and to some extent to steer the global integration of the higher education systems. Without such a framework the globalisation of higher education will be unrestrained and wild, generating a lot of resistance and protest.

Higher Education Market

One of the most visible manifestations of globalisation is the emerging 'borderless' higher education market. The huge increase in the worldwide demand in higher education, the budgetary and capacity problems of many nations to meet this demand, and the opportunities created by new communication technologies and the Internet, shape an environment in which new, mostly for-profit providers successfully can expand the supply of educational services. Universities from North America, Europe and Australia take initiatives to reach out their educational provision to this international higher education market, by active recruitment of international, fee-paying students to the home institution, by establishing branch campuses or franchising and twinning agreements with local institutions, or via distance education and e-learning and other transnational activities. The international demand for higher education has also invited new providers from outside the higher education sector to enter the scene.

The 'business of borderless education' comprises various forms and developments, among which also combinations are possible, such as new for-profit private universities, corporate 'universities', media companies delivering educational programmes, professional associations becoming directly active in higher education, and companies with high training needs establishing their own training facilities. Many of these new providers extensively use the Internet as delivery channel; in some cases they develop into real 'cyber-universities' with a very limited physical presence. Drifting away from the old academic culture of traditional universities – and sometimes even openly questioning it –, and blurring the distinctions between academic, research-driven education and vocational training, they defy the age-old identity of universities.

In some niches, such as business administration studies, their substantial growth poses a direct threat to the market position of existing traditional universities, although in many other sectors of mass delivery of initial higher education degrees their capacity to compete with the publicly funded institutions is very limited.

However, in some countries, mainly in Eastern Europe, the former Soviet Union and the developing world, their presence even on this level is substantial, due to insufficient domestic public supply and the growth of demand in middle classes willing to pay for higher education. Although there are also less reputable initiatives and real 'diploma mills', the reaction of national governments and traditional universities in some countries to these new providers is sometimes exaggerated. To some extent their development even enriches the higher education sector, awakes innovation also in the old institutions and challenges productively the academic tradition. Still, important issues of access and equity on the one hand and quality on the other are raised by the global rise of private, for-profit higher education.

COMMODIFICATION OF EDUCATION

To begin it is helpful to distinguish between the rise of the market, 'with its insidious consumer-based appropriations of freedom and choice' and its impact on education, and globalisation. They are wrapped up—one with another—but it has been possible to talk of the marketisation of education without having to refer to delocalisation and the activities of multinationals. Now, that is increasingly difficult.

As we know, commercial concerns look constantly for new markets and areas of activity. In the last quarter of the twentieth century, and particularly in those states where neo-liberal economic policies dominated, there was strong pressure to 'roll-back' state regulation, and to transform non-market and 'social' spheres such as public health and education services into arenas of commercial activity. According to Colin Leys, such a transformation—the making of a market—entailed the meeting of four requirements:

- The reconfiguration of the goods and services in question so that they can be priced and sold.
- The inducing of people to want to buy them.
- The transformation of the workforce from one working for collective aims with a service ethic to one working to produce profits for owners of capital and subject to market discipline.
- The underwriting of the risks to capital by the state.

What we have here is a process of commodification—and the development of attempts to standardise 'products' and to find economies of scale. The expansion of higher education in Britain and Northern Ireland during this period, for instance, involved a the restructuring of courses and programmes so that they could be marketed. This included marketing new courses such as MBAs, modulisation, and the increased use of part-time and distance learning programmes. The introduction of student loans and course fees has raised, significantly, the direct cost placed upon students—and helped to change people's orientation to higher education away from that of participants towards being consumers.

The massive increase in university enrollment was, however, less a consequence of government policy, than the impact of changing perceptions of the labour market. The surge in student numbers occurred because it became clear to large numbers of people that *not* having a degree disadvantaged them in the labour market.

At a certain point in what had been a steady, slow expansion, large numbers of people started to feel they really had better get a degree, because not doing so would be such a bad move. The first wave set off another and so on.

There has also been a transformation of the labour force in higher education—and a growing orientation to profit generation. Salary levels have decreased significant relative to other key groupings; increased bureaucratisation and pressures on universities to reduce costs have reduced the time for 'scholarship and disinterested learning' and the doubling in the numbers of students per lecturer has led to a progressive decline in the quality of teaching and the satisfaction it gives to learners and teachers. Similar pressures can be found at work in other areas of education.

We have also seen some very significant movements towards corporatisation in schooling and non-formal education. In the 1980s and early 1990s this was initially carried forward by the rise of managerialism in many 'western' education systems. Those in authority were encouraged and trained to see themselves as managers, and to reframe the problems of education as exercises in delivering the right outcomes. The language and disposition of management also quickly moved into the classroom via initiatives such as the national curriculum. There has also been the wholesale strengthening of the market in many education systems.

Schools have to compete for students in order to sustain and extend their funding. This, in turn, has meant that they have had to market their activities and to develop their own 'brands'. They have had to sell 'the learning experience' and the particular qualities of their institution. To do this complex processes have to be reduced to easily identified packages; philosophies to sound bites; and students and their parents become 'consumers'. As Stewart demonstrated some time ago there is a fundamental problem with the way that such business models have been applied to educational and welfare agencies.

The real danger is that unthinking adoption of the private sector model prevents the development of an approach to management in the public services in general or to the social services in particular based on their distinctive purposes, conditions and tasks. The result has been a drive towards to the achievement of specified outcomes and the adoption of standardised teaching models. The emphasis is less on community and equity, and rather more on individual advancement and the need to satisfy investors and influential consumers. Education has come to resemble a private, rather than public, good.

As might be expected, such marketisation and commodification has led to a significant privatisation of education in a number of countries. In the United States, for example, schooling, higher education and training have been seen as lucrative markets to be in. Giroux reports that the for-profit education market represented around $600 billion in revenue for corporate interests. Over 1000 state schools have been contracted out to private companies.

In Britain education management, 'looks like it is about to become big business'. Educational Action zones have had significant corporate involvement. The Lambeth Zone is run by Shell, for example, not the local education authority. In Southwark, the education service has been contracted out to Haskins, and Kings Manor School, Guildford became the first state school to have its administration has been handed to a private company

Seeking to turn education into a commodity, framing it in market terms, and encouraging the entry of commercial concerns could be seen as simply an expression of neo-liberal politics in a particular state or area. However, we need to understand the nature of the forces that have pushed governments into adopting such policies—and it is here that we can see the process of globalisation directly at work.

Globalisation has impacted upon the nature of the agencies that 'school' children, young people and adults. The question we are facing now is, To what extent is the educational endeavor affected by processes of globalisation that are threatening the autonomy of national educational systems and the sovereignty of the nation-state as the ultimate ruler in democratic societies? At the same time, how is globalisation changing the fundamental conditions of an educational system premised on fitting into a community, a community characterised by proximity and familiarity?

At first glance it would seem that national governments still have considerable freedom to intervene in education systems. Government, for example, has significantly increased the scale of central direction and intervention through the use of national curriculum requirements, special initiatives and other, institutional means. However, as soon as we examine the nature of this expansion of intervention we can see that the overriding concern is with economic growth and international competitiveness—and that the efforts of politicians have been deeply flawed and their record dismal.

While there is some direct intervention in the governance of national educational systems by trans-national agencies such as the IMF and World Bank, the impact of globalisation is most felt through the extent to which politics everywhere are now essentially market-driven. 'It is not just that governments can no longer "manage" their national economies', he comments, 'to survive in office they must increasingly "manage" national politics in such a ways as to adapt them to the pressures of trans-national market forces'.

DE-LOCALISATION AND CHANGING TECHNOLOGIES

As well as conditioning the political context, globalisation has found expression in some very direct ways—via , for example, the de-localisation of schooling. Since the 1980s, there has been a degree of 'parental choice; within state schooling. It has been possible to choose which schools to apply to at both primary and secondary levels. While much primary school application is local, a significant proportion of secondary school application is not. This has both severed the link between locality and schooling and undermined the idea of community schooling.

A further degree of delocalisation has occurred as a result of scares around child protection and truancy. While schools might be local, access to the neighbourhood and of neighbours to the school has been restricted. The most visible signs are the security gates and fences that are part of the perimeter of schooling. Such measures inevitably strengthen the idea that the school is somehow separate from the community where it is located—and this is further intensified by the regime of testing and centralised curriculum construction that has been the hallmark of the education system since the early 1980s. There has been significantly less room for more local community-oriented explorations and student projects. As we have seen, the main forces framing the centralised curriculum are economic and directly linked to globalisation.

To these developments must be added changes in educational technology—especially the use of the internet and other computer forms, and the growth of distance learning. At one level these can be seen as an instrument of localisation. They allow people to study at home or at work. However, they usually involve highly individualised forms of learning and may not lead to any additional interaction with neighbours or with local shops, agencies and groups. They also allow people from very different parts of the world to engage in the same programme—and student contact can be across great physical distance.

The term adult learning has been substituted for adult education in many policy and academic discussions in recognition of these sorts of shifts and more recently there has been a major growth in attention to notions of lifelong learning. The shift may, as Courtney suggests, reflect a growing interest in learning, 'however unorganised, episodic or experiential', beyond the classroom.

There has been a fundamental shift in the behaviour of 'ordinary citizens', 'who increasingly regard the day-to-day practice of adult learning as routine, perhaps so routine that they give it little explicit attention'. Economic, social and cultural changes mean that many now live in 'knowledge' or 'informational societies' that have strong individualising tendencies and a requirement for permanent learning reflexivity. As a result, Field goes on to suggest, many adults now take part in organised learning throughout their lifespan; that the post-school system is populated by adults as well as by young people; and that 'non-formal' learning permeates daily life and is valued.

Typical of the last of these has been a substantial increase in activities such as short residential courses, study tours, fitness centres, sports clubs, heritage centres, self-help therapy manuals, management gurus, electronic networks and self-instructional videos. In these latter examples we can see an important aspect of the growing trans-national corporate presence in education and learning—and the extent to which profits are dependent on people continuing and extending their self-directed learning projects and activities.

HIGHER EDUCATION AND CONSUMERISM

There are many ways of making money from formal education, 'but the most widespread is the use of the school as an advertising medium'. The attraction is obvious—schools represent a captive market. Through the use of teaching packs, sponsored videos, advertisements on school computer screen savers and the like, large companies are able to bring their brand directly into the classroom. In so doing they are looking to gain a certain legitimacy as well as the raising general brand awareness. Schools also have the distinct advantage for corporates of organising their students along key demographics such as age and supposed academic ability—so it is possible to target advertising and marketing. The shortfall of funding for key aspects of schooling such as computing, sport and recreational and eating facilities: fast-food, athletic gear and computing companies have stepped in.

Many teachers and their managers remain 'deeply ambivalent' about the movement of commerce and advertising into schools. There is a belief that children need at least one 'commercial-free zone'. Students in many northern counties are, generally, 'intense consumers'. They are prepared to and/or want to 'spend large amounts of money on brand names and fashionable and popular items'. However, while many may be critical of certain aspects of consumer culture, they are far less likely to be critical of consumption itself.

As educational systems become more marketised, colleges, schools and non-formal education agencies seeks to build relationships based more on viewing learners as customers rather than participants The main role of the teacher-turned-classroom manager is to legitimate through mandated subject matter and educational practices a market-based conception of the learner as simply a consumer of information. The result of this incursion by commerce, and the widespread seeping of managerialism, market-thinking and consumerism into the orientation of educators is a basic inability within many schooling systems and agencies of informal education to address critically questions around globalisation, branding and consumption.

HIGHER EDUCATION AND WTO

Higher education is increasingly seen as a commercial product to be bought and sold like any other commodity. Higher education commercialisation has now reached the global marketplace. The World Trade Organisation (WTO) is considering a series of proposals to include higher education as one of its concerns, ensuring that the import and export of higher education be subject to the complex rules and legal arrangements of the WTO protocols and free of most restrictions. In the United States, the National Committee for International Trade in Education and a group of mainly for-profit education providers are supporting this initiative. The established higher education community, including the American Council on Education, is not involved in this undertaking.

The WTO initiative poses a severe threat to the traditional ideals of the university, as well as to the national and even institutional control of education, and therefore needs careful scrutiny. We are in the midst of a true revolution in higher education, a revolution that has the potential to profoundly change our basic understanding of the role of the university. The implications are immense and as yet little discussed or understood. It is especially alarming, but not surprising, that the U.S. Department of Commerce's Office of Service Industries is behind the effort to commercialise higher education in the United States and worldwide.

Higher education institutions everywhere are subject to global trends—massification and all of its implications, the impact of the new communications technologies, accountability of academic institutions to government, an increasingly international and mobile academic profession, global research networks, and other phenomena.

Many of these developments link academic institutions and systems globally. The use of English as the lingua franca for scientific communication and for teaching, especially when combined with the Internet, makes communication easier and quicker. The advent of multinational higher education institutions makes it possible to disseminate new curricular and other innovations quickly and to meet the immediate needs of students and the national economies of countries that lack adequate providers of higher education.

For centuries, universities were seen as institutions that provided education in the learned professions and scientific disciplines. Universities, as independent and sometimes critical institutions, preserved and interpreted, and sometimes expanded, the history and culture of society. In the 19th century, research was added to the responsibilities of the universities, followed a little later by service to society. Academic institutions were, in the main, sponsored by the state or the church. Even privately sponsored institutions were defined by the service mission. Higher education was seen as a "public good," as something that provided a valuable contribution to society and was therefore worthy of support.

Universities were places for learning, research, and service to society through the application of knowledge. Academe was afforded a significant degree of insulation from the pressures of society—academic freedom—precisely because it was serving the broader good of society. Professors were often given permanent appointments—tenure—to guarantee them academic freedom in the classroom and laboratory to teach and do research without fear of sanctions from society.

Today, trends such as the rise of the Internet and the globalisation of knowledge have the potential for creating severe problems for academic institutions and systems in smaller or poorer nations. In a world divided into centers and peripheries, the centers grow stronger and more dominant and the peripheries become increasingly marginalised. Inequalities grow more pronounced. There is little leeway for academic systems or individual universities to independently develop in the increasingly competitive and fast moving global higher education scene dominated by the world-class universities in the industrialised countries. The traditional academic center becomes ever stronger and more dominant–mainly in the English-speaking countries of the North (the United States, the United Kingdom, Canada) and in Australia, and in the larger countries of the European Union.

The norms, values, language, scientific innovations, and knowledge products of countries in the center crowd out other ideas and practices. These countries are home not only to the dominant universities and research facilities but also to the multinational corporations so powerful in the new global knowledge system. Information technology companies such as Microsoft and IBM, biotechnology and pharmaceutical firms (Merck or Biogen), multinational publishers like Elsevier or Bertelsmann, among others, dominate the new international commerce in knowledge, knowledge-based products, and information technology. Smaller and poorer countries have little autonomy or competitive potential in the globalised world. Globalisation in higher education exacerbates dramatic inequalities among the world's universities.

With the growing commercialisation of higher education, the values of the marketplace have intruded onto the campus. One of the main factors is the change in society's attitude toward higher education—which is now seen as a "private good" benefiting those who study or do research. In this view, it seems justified that the users should pay for this service as they would for any other service. The provision of knowledge becomes just another commercial transaction. The main provider of public funds, the state, is increasingly unwilling or unable to provide the resources needed for an expanding higher education sector.

Universities and other post-secondary institutions are expected to generate more of their funding. They have had to think more like businesses and less like educational institutions. In this context a logical development is the privatisation of public universities—the selling of knowledge products, partnering with corporations, as well as increases in student fees. The proliferation of private academic institutions of all kinds, especially in the for-profit sector, is another by-product of commercialisation. Education companies, some of which call themselves universities, sell skills and training, awarding degrees or certificates to customers (students). Research is seen as a fungible product rather than an inquiry conducted to advance the frontiers of science.

In these changed circumstances, it is not surprising that those motivated by commerce, in government and in the private sector, would concern themselves with ensuring that "knowledge products" are freely traded in the international marketplace. If these interest groups have their way, higher education in all of its manifestations will be subject to free trade discipline just like bananas or airliners.

The rules of the WTO, and its related General Agreement on Trade and Services (GATS), it must be remembered, are legally binding. There is a danger that regulations relating to higher education will be included in an international agreement "under the radar" and without much analysis. When something becomes part of the WTO regime requirements and regulations, it is subject to complex arrangements. The implications for higher education are immense, not only because of a new set of international regulations but because the university will be defined in an entirely new way: the overriding goal of GATS and the WTO is to guarantee market access to educational products and institutions of all kinds.

The trade in higher education is, of course, more difficult to codify than bananas. But efforts are now under way to do precisely this – to create a regime of guidelines and regulations to institute free trade in higher education. The WTO would help to guarantee that academic institutions or other education providers could set up branches in any country, export degree programmes, award degrees and certificates with minimal restriction, invest in overseas educational institutions, employ instructors for their foreign ventures, set up educational and training programmes through distance technologies without controls, and so on.

Educational products of all kinds would be freely exported from one country to another. Copyright, patent, and licensing regulations, already part of international treaties, would be further reinforced. It would become very difficult to regulate the trade in academic institutions, programmes, degrees, or products across international borders. Those wishing to engage in such imports and exports would have recourse to international tribunals and legal action. At present the jurisdiction over higher education is entirely in the hands of national authorities.

The questions raised by this initiative relate to the very idea of higher education and to the future of academe especially in the developing nations and in smaller countries. How would countries, or individual universities, maintain their academic independence in a world in which they had minimal practical and legal control over the import or export of higher education? How would accreditation or quality control be carried out? Would there be a distinction made between public or private nonprofit higher education – the "gold standard" for centuries – and the new and aggressive for-profit sector? Would wealthy profit-driven multinationals force other higher education institutions out of business?

Would a full-time professoriate with claims to academic freedom survive? One thing is very clear—once the universities are part of the WTO jurisdiction, autonomy would be severely compromised and advanced education and research would become just another product subject to international treaties and bureaucratic regulations.

The greatest negative impact of WTO control over higher education would occur in the developing countries. These countries have the greatest need for academic institutions that can contribute to national development, produce research relevant to local needs, and participate in the strengthening of civil society. Once universities in developing countries are subject to an international academic marketplace regulated by the WTO, they would be swamped by overseas institutions and programmes intent on earning a profit but not in contributing to national development. It is not clear that accrediting and quality control mechanisms that now exist in many countries would be permitted, at least as they relate to transnational educational providers.

Every country needs to maintain essential control over its academic institutions. At the same time, individual universities need an adequate degree of autonomy and academic freedom if they are to flourish. For centuries, traditional universities have performed a central function in society. While that function has changed over time, it has not disappeared. The challenge of the new initiatives and globalisation generally is one of the most serious since the medieval universities faced the rise of nationalism and the Protestant Reformation in the 16th century. For almost a millennium, universities have defined themselves as institutions with a core educational mission and a common understanding of the values of academe. For much of this period, universities were understood not only as institutions that provided education in practical fields of knowledge but as central cultural institutions in society. In the 19th century, science and research were added to the academic mission. Universities were recognised as special institutions by society precisely because their goals went beyond everyday commerce. Now, all of this is under threat.

The academic community itself is in considerable part responsible for the changes. Some universities have all too willingly allowed themselves to be caught up in commercial activities and to compromise their traditional roles. The establishment of "for-profit" subsidiaries by such renowned institutions as New York University and Columbia University is symbolic of these compromises. Monash University, a well-known Australian institution, is establishing profit making branches overseas. The University of Chicago's business school has opened branches in Spain and Singapore. Universities in China devote much of their attention to providing profit-making consulting and setting up technology companies. Many universities have gone "on-line" to sell their courses and degrees to customers in all parts of the world.

If universities are to survive as intellectual institutions, they must pay close attention to their core responsibilities of teaching, learning, and research. Maintaining loyalty to traditional academic values will not be easy, but the costs of growing commercialisation are much greater.

Governments and other public authorities need to give the universities the support they need to fulfil their mission. Constantly squeezing the budget, demanding ever greater accountability, and insisting that the university fundamentally change its goals does not in the long run serve the public interest. The public must also respect the underlying values of higher education.

The developing countries have special academic needs that must be protected, and any WTO-style treaty would inevitably harm the emerging academic systems of the developing countries. Third World universities are now involved in many international relationships, but these arrangements are based on national needs and allow choice among programmes and partners.

The proposed WTO initiatives bring all of the pressures now being felt by universities worldwide into sharp focus. If higher education worldwide were subject to the strictures of the WTO, academe would be significantly altered. The idea that the university serves a broad public good would be weakened, and the universities would be subject to all of the commercial pressures of the marketplace—a marketplace enforced by international treaties and legal requirements. The goal of having the university contribute to national development and the strengthening of civil society in developing countries would be impossible to fulfil. Universities are indeed special institutions with a long history and a societal mission that deserve support. Subjecting academe to the rigours of a WTO-enforced marketplace would destroy one of the most valuable institutions in any society.

NEED FOR A REGULATORY FRAMEWORK

The developments described above surely will have a profound impact on the higher education system worldwide, even if there are many unknown elements and the exact size of some trends remains unclear. The massive character of the developments and the fact that they escape the well-known regulatory frameworks at institutional and national policy levels impede the development of a coherent position from the higher education community. However, the impact of globalisation on higher education generates a number of crucial challenges, which ask for a new and international regulatory framework.

Regulation of New Providers

A first challenge concerns the regulation of new providers and the various forms of transnational higher education. There are huge differences in the way countries are dealing with private universities, for-profit providers and transnational higher education. In some countries – Greece and Israel can stand as examples – there is an almost total refusal to include those non-national providers in the national higher education system or to recognise their diplomas and degrees. Other countries, especially in the developing world, recognise the incapacity to meet the increasing demand by their domestic providers and welcome foreign providers.

One can say that in most countries the traditional viewpoint still is that higher education is a public responsibility, that institutions have to be publicly recognised and financed, and that it is the national state that gives formal public validity to their degrees, leaving not much space to private and foreign providers. The notion 'public' is solely identified with 'national'; thus, institutions which are seen as public in their mother country, become private when engaging in transnational activities in other countries. The distinction public-private, which has been perceived as essential in higher education policy for such a long time, becomes very blurred in the age of globalisation.

In principle, there is no reason to oppose a more positive and open attitude towards private and transnational higher education, even when defending a 'public good' approach to higher education. In modern policy approaches the idea must be accepted that private and non-national institutions can also fulfil public functions. Although the traditional higher education institutions have a tradition and specific academic culture and value-system to defend, it should be strong enough to engage in a more competitive situation with providers coming from another background. The monopoly created by national policy frameworks, which undoubtedly has some 'protectionist' aspects, is not a promising environment to tackle future challenges. Moreover, this policy debate risks to be overruled by the tendencies to see transnational higher education merely as a trade issue, in need of liberalisation.

Some observers see the future in a completely liberalised global higher education market, where national authorities and traditional universities no longer will be able to 'protect' their markets and impose their values on students and society. Even if such views still seem to be rather marginal, the factual policy context will change dramatically if the proposals in the WTO to include higher education services in the GATS are adopted, since then 'knowledge services' can be freely traded in the global marketplace.

Since these proposals enjoy intensive lobbying from the for-profit providers, are backed by the US government and receive also support from some developing nations seeing it as an opportunity to increase the supply of higher education in their countries, it is likely that they will be realised. Even if formally public provision of higher education will be exempted, marketisation and increasing competition in the international higher education market will be the consequences of liberalisation, further eroding the 'public good' approach in higher education and the traditional academic culture in universities.

For the potential student and the general public, the situation will not be very clear and transparent; the actual value of qualifications delivered by private and foreign providers will remain unclear in most countries, even the question on which grounds institutions can label themselves 'universities' will be very difficult to answer.

However, a solely defensive reaction, falling back to traditional and exclusively national regulation to support a 'public good' approach and to guarantee open access and 'consumer' protection, protecting the domestic public higher education sector, would be very conservative, short-sighted and ineffective.

What is needed is a truly international and sustainable policy framework for dealing with private and transnational providers, reconciling the interests of national governments, the traditional public higher education sector, for-profit providers and the needs of the demand side of students and the general public interest. It is very important from the start to stress that such a framework is distinct from and comes before the more ambitious quality assurance and accreditation framework. This framework should transcend the basic requirements imposed by national and international trade and commerce laws and regulations, but should refrain also from becoming a comprehensive and complicated bureaucratic procedure of 'recognition'. It should have the ambition to cover physical transnational education as well as virtual delivery via the Internet. Minimally, this international regulatory framework should contain:

- an international glossary of common concepts, definitions and terminology,
- some basic rules to grant providers the 'licence to teach',
- an internationally standardised procedure of registration,
- some rules concerning the correct use of the basic labels such as 'university', 'doctorate', 'professor', 'master degree', 'accredited', etc.,
- the removal of existing barriers to mobility of students and staff, not dealt with in international trade agreements,

- some basic elements of a professional code of good practice,
- a basic arrangement of the intellectual property issues associated with private higher education, and
- an agreement on issues of consumer protection and rights of complaint.

Private and transnational providers should perceive it as in their own interest to actively and positively engage in the realisation of such a regulatory framework. Moreover, in addition to the international regulatory framework the combined public and private higher education sector should be stimulated to establish their own self-regulation, in order to rule out bad practice and to eliminate charlatans, rogue providers and untrustworthy diploma mills, so that they can build a worldwide trust and esteem as respectable service sector. Necessary for this are strong associations of higher education institutions, both of the traditional academic universities and of new, for-profit providers.

Finding Solution for International Transferability

A second and not at all new challenge is finding a comprehensive solution for the issue of the international transferability and recognition of qualifications and credits. This issue has two sub-questions which in fact are merely two sides of the same problem, namely the recognition of foreign diplomas and degrees and the recognition of diplomas and degrees delivered by non-recognised institutions.

During the last decade some important initiatives have been taken by a number of international organisations, mainly in Europe (UNESCO, CEPES, Council of Europe, European Commission, etc.), and the so-called Lisbon Convention is an important step forward, exchanging the old concept of equivalence to that of a more flexible recognition. Nevertheless, in a context of growing mobility of skilled labour and globalisation of the professions, the rather strict national regulations concerning recognition of qualifications create many problems and frequent unnecessary insecurity and suffering for individuals and families.

The enormous diversity in national higher education systems and degree architecture is still mirrored by complicated bureaucratic procedures to investigate whether a foreign or unknown degree matches the domestic ones. Even countries defending a liberalisation of higher education trade, such as the US, apply very strict and severe procedures for the validation of foreign degrees in their own country.

Backing this conservative and bureaucratic attitude is not only the will to protect the own, well-known institutions, but also an often unrealistic appreciation of the quality of the domestic degrees, not checked by a truly objective comparative understanding of the value of and diversity in foreign degrees. Even if an understanding of the impact of globalisation on higher education and mobility of professional labour would call for a truly international approach, radically breaking with the national control over recognition of qualifications, it is unrealistic to expect that national authorities will be willing to give up this crucial competence. It is regrettable that apparently this issue cannot be resolved within the field of educational policy, and that it has to be circumvented by policies regarding professional mobility, as is the case in the European Union and also in the context of NAFTA.

The professions, which are more and more organised on an international scale - as is the case with for example engineering, medicine, accounting and many others - are ready to adopt more flexible attitudes in this matter than most national authorities. In this field some important international agreements, such as the Washington Accord in the field of engineering and technology, pave the way for an international approach.

A perhaps less important, but similar problem concerns the recognition of study periods and credits obtained abroad or in non-recognised institutions. Also within programmes there increasingly is mobility, promoted by programmes such as ERASMUS / SOCRATES in the European Union. In the US and between countries that have adopted a similar system, there is at least a common definition of what a credit represents.

In the European Union the ECTS is generalising as an exchange device, although there also are proposals within the context of the Bologna process to develop it into a real credit transfer and accumulation system, even encompassing lifelong learning credits. The development of modular courses and the evolution towards less standardised and more flexible curricula will increase the importance of credits as units for validation of learning experiences. The growing interest in recognition of experiential learning in higher education and lifelong learning even will call for a definition of credits, which is independent of formal learning, as is still the case in both the American and European concepts of credit. The transferability of such credits over national boundaries will not be easy, when many countries even refuse to recognise formal academic study in institutions beyond their administrative supervision.

Some experts expect that focusing on the outcomes of education and learning, thus leaving behind the evaluation of the formal inputs in the learning process, can resolve this issue. It is interesting to see that there are such developments in the field of vocational training, for example in France with the *centres de bilan de compétences*. In the field of higher education however, there is some interest in shifting the focus to outcomes and competencies, but no general willingness to make a complete abstraction of the formal aspects of the educational experience.

Other experts think that the issue of recognition of degrees and credits will automatically be resolved with the development of international accreditation systems. It is however unlikely that a general framework of international accreditation will be realised in the short run and that countries automatically will accept the consequences of it for the recognition of qualifications. This strategy would leave mobile graduates and students in the cold for an unacceptable long period of time.

Thus, there is no alternative than to take a new international initiative in the field of recognition of qualifications. The higher education sector and the national educational authorities have to be convinced that the issue is serious and pressing, that it is not wise to leave this issue to the courts, that the regulation in the field of professional recognition leads to an erosion of educational competences, and that they have to take up the responsibility to find a common, international approach themselves. The growing harmonisation and integration of higher education systems, degree structures and curricula among countries joining a common 'higher education area' eventually create a more positive environment for higher education institutions and national authorities to move to a more flexible attitude in this field. International associations and organisations can take some concrete steps to facilitate this process.

The outcome of the process should be no less than a more or less automatic recognition of foreign degrees and credits within 'higher education areas' with similar higher education systems and quality assurance procedures. To include degrees delivered by non-recognised private providers, some additional measures have to be taken on top of those suggested in point 1. There has to be some kind of international 'recognition' of the institution or institutional accreditation, and the programme concerned should be subject to the same quality assurance and accreditation procedures as those applied to the already recognised institutions and programmes.

Developing an Approach to Quality Assurance

The third and probably most important challenge of course is developing an international approach to quality assurance and accreditation. In the previous decade quality assurance and accreditation systems in higher education have been developed in many countries. By far the most of them are national schemes, oriented to the domestic higher education systems. As a consequence, transnational activities of universities and especially distance education and e-learning activities in many cases are not covered by these national quality assurance and accreditation schemes. Since there is a great variety in and limited international communication on standards and benchmarking, the readability and transparency of these quality assurance and accreditation systems to other countries, foreign institutions and international students is low, and therefore the relevance of these national schemes in the context of globalisation of higher education is limited as well.

In a number of countries accreditation schemes have been developed as an instrument to regulate and control the higher education market. There is no generally accepted definition of accreditation in higher education, and in many cases the term is used also to indicate procedures of recognition of institutions, ex ante authorisation or licensing of programmes of new providers, approval of nationally controlled curricula, etc. Here, we use a rather pragmatic definition of accreditation, namely the formal and public statement by an external body, resulting from a quality assurance procedure, that agreed standards of quality are met by an institution or programme.

An accredited status can have specific consequences, for example regarding the degree-awarding capacity, the recognition of those degrees, funding, credit-transfer, access to postgraduate programmes in third institutions, etc. The situation with regard to accreditation internationally is very diverse, with the differences mainly concentrating on the issue of the role of the state in accreditation. In some countries, such as the US, voluntary accreditation of institutions has a long tradition. The American example has led to the development of accreditation in many other countries, but mostly driven by the national authorities willing to control the domestic higher education market. In Europe accreditation is a much debated issue in the context of the Bologna process and opinions are divided, with countries moving to various kinds of accreditation schemes and others opposing it, some institutions seeing it as a necessary instrument to guarantee quality and to differentiate the market and others seeing it as an intolerable attack on their autonomy.

It is clear that, a Dutch-Flemish experiment excepted, there is a strict national focus in the European debate on accreditation and a resistance against any form of transnational accreditation system. And those who think about international accreditation, sometimes see it as a strategy to differentiate a specific group of countries or institutions from those outside, and thus to create new divisions. This is often also the case with networks of universities developing mutual inter-institutional accreditation procedures. This short overview illustrates that inter- or transnational accreditation virtually is non-existing and that sometimes accreditation even is used to protect the domestic higher education market and to counteract the development of private and transnational higher education.

The establishment of transnational professional accreditation compensates the absence of truly inter- or transnational public accreditation systems to some extent. Already clearly developed in the fields of engineering (ABET) and management studies (EQUIS), but in development in other professions, these schemes of international professional accreditation fill in the gap left by the national authorities and the higher education community.

Another development is the import of foreign accreditors, as is the case of American accreditors or the British Open University validation scheme asked to accredit programmes or institutions in other countries. The establishment of organisations specifically devoted to the accreditation of transnational accreditation is another interesting case, although up to now the most important endeavour in this field, GATE, has not be very successful due to its links with a particular for-profit provider.

These developments have in common that they originated outside the higher education community and policy fields, demonstrating the inability of the global higher education world itself to develop its own systems of transnational self-regulation. They also indicate that international accreditation is becoming a reality, although external to the international higher education community itself, and that institutions in the future will be facing a situation of 'multiple accreditation' coming from various origins.

There is a growing agreement on the viewpoint that globalisation in higher education urgently asks for a transnational approach to quality assurance and accreditation, but there are huge differences of vision on how to achieve this and which steps have to be taken. A minimal strategy is to improve communication and exchange among national quality assurance agencies, in the hope that this will lead to a kind of harmonisation and international benchmarking of trustworthy standards and methodologies and the gradual mutual recognition of agencies and schemes. This minimal strategy, defended for example by ENQA, legitimating the quality assurance and accreditation competencies of the national states, risks to take too much time and to remain too voluntaristic in the light of the profound and accelerating impact of globalisation.

A second strategy is to develop a kind of soft validation and approval procedure for existing quality assurance and accreditation systems. International associations such as IAUP think of the possibility to establish a clearinghouse of trustworthy quality assurance and accreditation systems in the world, based on a mutually accepted definition of concepts and basic standards and criteria.

Following on this, a third strategy could be the development of real meta-accreditation on an international scale. There are no real significant examples of this for the moment and it is difficult to imagine where such an initiative would derive the authority and legitimacy from to take up a well-defined and trustworthy position in the field. However, the fact that some international professional accreditation schemes succeed in establishing their authority suggests that in principle it would be possible also for the international higher education community to do the same. International organisations such as UNESCO could provide the moral authority and legitimacy to start some experiments in this area.

A fourth strategy, the development of a real international accreditation agency, seems to be very unrealistic for the moment, given the unwillingness of national states to transfer that kind of crucial competence to an international agency, but also because many fear that this will lead to a very bureaucratic, costly apparatus escaping any kind of control from governments and higher education institutions.

There is no doubt that this issue asks for urgent consideration and action on an international level. The impact of globalisation is such that without a trustworthy international quality scheme of whatever kind that could balance the development of the global higher education market, we will have to face severe problems in the future of which especially the countries in the less developed parts of the world and their students will be the victims. It is difficult to underestimate the risks associated with various kinds of rogue providers and diploma mills.

Growing insecurity about the quality status of foreign degrees will lead to even more severe checks at the level of national governments and a more protectionist attitude among institutions, creating more problems regarding recognition of qualifications and mobility of professional labour that those already existing today, and further inhibiting that development of transnational higher education. It is in the self-interest of the global higher education community to develop transnational quality assurance and accreditation systems that can counterbalance the globalisation of higher education.

As a start it is worthwhile to consider some initial steps:

- an agreement on a common set of definitions and a glossary of concepts regarding international quality assurance and accreditation;
- an agreement on a basic set of principles, a.o. that quality assurance and accreditation primarily are a kind of self-regulation of the higher education system, that accreditation is only possible on the basis of existing quality assurance experiences, that international accreditation must respect institutional autonomy and diversity;
- an initiative to convince the international higher education community, its key actors and its associations that it has to develop transnational forms of self-regulation with respect to quality itself, at the risk of giving away the initiative in this crucial issue;
- an initiative to national authorities to convince them to seek international cooperation in the field of quality assurance and accreditation;
- an initiative to seek the cooperation of the internationally organised professions in the development of an international regulatory framework with regard to quality assurance and accreditation;
- start of work by experts on the analysis and evaluation of standards, criteria and benchmarking procedures used in existing quality assurance and accreditation systems, in order to investigate the possibility of the definition of internationally agreed minimum standards.

3

PRIVATISATION OF HIGHER EDUCATION

Privatisation suggests a movement away from public financing and toward private financing. For higher education, the term includes a range of activities taking place on campus. Generally, in the name of financial necessity, colleges and universities cut services, undertake aggressive outsourcing, reduce the number of regular tenured teaching slots, and increase tuition. This takes place against a background of state-defined accountability standards as legislators take a more assertive role in setting education goals. Privatisation includes more centralised decision making, declining acceptance of academic norms, loss of faculty autonomy, and developing private funding sources.

The trend toward privatisation has been associated with an historical shift in the population served by higher education. Traditionally, colleges and universities were understood as experiences for an elite few, but, increasingly, they have become a normal part of the educational experience of larger and more diverse student populations. This evolution from elite to mass accessibility has resulted in higher education more closely resembling a public utility than an experience reserved for privileged elites.

The shift to higher education as public service has resulted in legislators treating it like any other public utility: they demand the most effective service at the most affordable price. The language used to define "effective" and "affordable" derives from a business model for generating value, where value is linked directly to short-term monetary gain. This redefines the traditional understanding of higher education's value, where value is linked directly to the long-term welfare of communities made up of informed citizens actively participating in the democratic process.

Privatisation increases the pressure on traditional higher education institutions to operate more efficiently, to pursue goals set by outside interests, and to market more aggressively. While such efforts can help an institution financially, they can also weaken collegial, knowledge-driven academic culture through the adoption of management practices more typical of business culture. Practices such as contracting out services and restructuring workforces represent market-driven attempts to control payroll, diversify and stabilise revenue, and shift costs to consumers.

Colleges and universities use outside vendors to provide a wide range of services. Most colleges indicate they are considering outsourcing even more services. The top five reasons colleges cite for contracting outside vendors include financial, quality improvement, equipment, human resources and staffing solutions, and safety/liability measures. Restructuring the workforce and controlling payroll. Most new full-time faculty positions in higher education are not tenureeligible.

Shared governance is a system in which those affected by the decisions participate in the decision making. In colleges, shared governance includes governing boards, administration, and faculty, with the participation of staff and students. This approach recognises the contributions and requirements of all members in a group consensus process. The results of this approach may include empowerment, equal partnership, and a vested interest in successful outcomes. This is at the heart of the academic tradition and supports the faculty's role in shaping institutional policies and programmes. Erosion of faculty participation in decision making is one possible result of restructuring the higher education *workforce*.

Diversifying revenue streams and stabilising income. In the past, education was place bound. With few exceptions, students had to come to campus to take classes, and colleges could count on maintaining the market because of the huge development costs necessary to build a new campus. That geographic protection is challenged by the maturation of computer technology and the Internet, making it possible to deliver college courses anywhere at any time.

More typically, technology supports a hybrid model of web-enhanced education that allows a college or university to rent a classroom, hire some part-time faculty members, and deliver a canned class at a very low price to whomever enrols. These colleges centralise library holdings, student records, student aid processes, and other administrative functions on a web-based system. The price of entry into a new higher education community is negligible.

The portable college can offer courses and programmes with a large potential enrolment, targeting students who otherwise might attend traditional colleges in the region. Many, but not all, such colleges are operated as for profit enterprises. They receive no funding from states, but utilise student aid packages to attract students. While portable colleges will not replace traditional colleges, they will and do compete for students among place-bound colleges. This new class of institution adds to the market pressures on traditional higher education institutions.

Contract training and other entrepreneurial efforts represent additional strategies, not only for diversifying revenue streams but also for stabilising income. These efforts include counteracting unpredictable state support by shifting the focus of institutions away from the core educational mission toward efforts at revenue enhancement. Again, the priority of economic objectives displaces the academy's traditional goals. The effect of shifting attention toward other revenue sources is to take time and attention away from the core functions of the institution.

Shifting costs to consumers. We are reallocating public funding for higher education away from support to institutions and toward individual student aid. The admissions office, business office, and student aid office have grown in importance on every campus, and business concepts and their expression—such as market share, efficient pricing, and the student as customer have crept into the enrolment conversation. Loans have increased as an overall share of the student aid package, which can serve to make students acutely aware of the need for immediate employment upon graduation to pay them back. Because it can affect students' institutional choices—as well as their decisions about whether to pursue a liberal arts education—this dynamic amplifies the increasingly market-driven character of higher education.

FORCES SPREADING PRIVATISATION

The first force that is spurring the spread of privatisation in higher education is the rise of an information-based economy. Now the sources of wealth come from knowledge and communication instead of natural resources and physical labour, which once characterised the United States as an industrial society. This is a global rather than a national economy. The New Economy puts a premium on intellectual capital and the people who produce it. This means that the demand for higher education is expanding dramatically. Education is needed throughout a lifetime, and the marketplace for that education is international. This growth makes education appealing to the private sector.

Second, the demographics of higher education have changed substantially. Students above age 25, women, working adults, and part-time attenders accounted for most of the enrolment growth in the 1980s and 1990s. Less than a fifth of today's college students meet the traditional stereotype of attending school full time. For the new majority of students, higher education is not as central to their lives as it was for previous generations of students. Research shows they want a very different relationship with their college than students have historically had. They are looking for just four things: convenience, service, quality, and low cost. They are unwilling to pay for activities and services they do not use. What they are asking for is a stripped-down version of higher education minus the plethora of electives and student activities. They are prime candidates for adult-oriented, for-profit institutions, such as the University of Phoenix, which offer limited majors, few electives, and instruction by part-time faculty at convenient hours for students with great customer service in nearby locations in the suburbs and the business districts of our cities. They are also excellent candidates for for-profit or not-for-profit distance learning programmes that are available in their homes or at their offices at any hour.

Changes in the demographics of traditional students will also affect the future of higher education. The number of 18-year-olds is growing at the rate of more than 1 percent per year. However, the growth is occurring disproportionately in the South and the West. In addition, an increasing proportion of high school graduates are now attending college – currently 65 percent, compared with 42 percent in 1970. The result is a tidal wave of new enrolments coming to higher education and varying dramatically by state.

Third, higher education is being subjected to greater criticism than in the past on issues varying from low productivity and high cost to the quality of leadership and the inadequacy of technology use. This is an invitation to a private sector that rightly or wrongly sees higher education as the next health care industry.

A fourth force is the advent of new technologies, the nation's love affair with the Internet, and the growth of enormous capital for investment. Higher education is an appealing investment for the private sector. Not only is it perceived as troubled and slow to change, but it also generates an enormous amount of cash and its market is increasing and growing global. "Customers," better known as students, make long-term purchases lasting two to four or even more years, thereby providing a very dependable cash flow and revenue stream. Enrolment in higher education is also counter-cyclical, which is very unusual in a business.

College and university enrollments, translated as dollars, grow when the economy is bad because people are more likely to go to college when they cannot find work and to drop out at a greater rate when there are more jobs. On top of all of this, states and the federal government subsidise the higher education industry through their financial aid programmes. It's a terrific package. The results have been impressive. Venture capital firms with an interest in education are increasing substantially. Many major investment houses are developing higher education practices.

The convergence of knowledge organisations is a fifth force. Television and cable networks, publishers, symphony orchestras, public libraries, universities, and museums, among others, are all starting to engage in the very same activities. Each of these organisations is in the content business, whether that content is packaged as books, television shows, concerts, exhibits, or courses. What each is now attempting to do is to expand the audience for its content and the number and kinds of venues for distributing that content.

Finally, public trust in government has declined in recent years. The result is declining confidence in the non-profit sector and rising confidence in the for-profit sector.

CHALLENGES OF PRIVATISATION

The twenty-first century has brought with it profound challenges to the nature, values, and control of higher educations. Societal expectations and public resources for higher education are undergoing fundamental shifts. Changes both within and outside the academy are altering its character - its students, faculty, governance, curriculum, functions, and very place in society. Crisis and change in higher education "have been the rule, not the exception." Nevertheless, current changes are transforming higher education to an extent perhaps greater than since the end of World War II. A common thread runs through these issues: challenges to the content of colleges' and universities' "social contract." These challenges are apparent in ongoing conflicts over public and private benefits of higher education, equity and merit, undergraduate and graduate education, "basic" and commercially oriented research, or institutional autonomy and public control.

States today have become "minority partners" in the colleges and universities that typically bear their names. On average, states now supply only a little over one-third of public colleges' revenues. Yet because these funds generally pay most basic instructional costs, such as faculty and staff salaries, state support remains critical to public institutions. Over the next decade, a combination of acute state revenue constraints, competing demands for state resources, and ongoing changes in public attitudes toward higher education will likely result in continued shrinking and unpredictable state support for higher education. Although many private colleges are also facing serious budget difficulties due to rising costs, market limits on tuition increases, reduced private giving, and declining endowment income, public institutions, which generally have less ability to tap private sources, will be hit harder.

Shrinking State Funding

Because higher education is the largest discretionary item in states' budgets, state funding for higher education tends to rise when the economy and resulting state revenues are good and to drop during recessions. Even during boom times, funding may be less than it appears once inflation and rising enrolments are taken into account. During the economic recession of the early 1990s, states cut higher education appropriations by amounts unequalled in constant dollars since at least World War II, despite enrolment growth. In the late 1990s, state funding per student finally began returning to pre-1990 levels – only to be cut almost immediately during the recession early in the new century. .

Long-term prospects for state higher education funding are not favourable. Many experts believe that states' revenue problems will persist even after the economy improves because state tax systems are obsolete – for example, a growing percentage of economic activity is in non-taxed services and Internet sales – and because voter-imposed limits have made raising revenues more difficult. At the same time, an estimated 40-50 percent of state expenditures is locked up in mandated programme costs. These mandated costs are expected to increase, which already consumes about 20 percent of state budgets, as the rising numbers of the elderly require more health services. Also, state actions taken during economic boom times, such as tax cuts or implementation of popular new programmes, are hard to eliminate when the economy weakens.

In this environment of restricted revenues and mandated expenditures, higher education funding is a tempting target to cut, not only because it is discretionary but also because colleges, unlike many other state programmes, can tap other revenue sources, and because a growing proportion of the public believes that students should pay more of their college costs. Unpredictable state funding is equally problematic.

Unexpected cuts made during the academic year, after faculty have been hired, programmes put in place, and student fees set, leave institutions with difficult choices. Declining capital dollars for funding to construct, renovate, and maintain classroom or research buildings and campus infrastructure may be as big a constraint on institutions' ability to accommodate enrolment growth, recruit faculty, and conduct research as are state appropriations for operating expenses.

As institutions seek to offset declining state dollars, public colleges and universities are becoming increasingly "privatised." While the declining proportion of state funding at some institutions is due in part to success in obtaining more extramural grants and private donations as well as growth in auxiliary enterprises, nationally two-thirds of the change reflects the substitution of tuition and fee income in place of state support.

Many public institutions are themselves pursuing privatisation as a means to raise revenues or reallocate scarce state dollars. Some institutions are requiring that certain academic programmes, especially high-demand, high-return professional programmes like law or business, become fully or nearly fully funded by clients (students), business, or other private sources. Many law and business schools became fully self-supporting by 2004, and many other public research universities have been exploring similar moves; most already charged business, law, and medical students much higher fees than those charged other students.

Even teacher or school administrator training programmes have been privatised in some cases. While institution often want to use the state dollars "saved" for programmes less able to charge high fees, the result in some cases may be a further decrease in state funds. Institutions are pursuing other strategies as well. Many are expanding self-supporting part-time degree programmes geared to working professionals.

Community colleges and other institutions are expanding contract education programmes with specific businesses or industries. Both public and private universities have adopted commercial technology transfer and other for-profit collaborations with industry. Colleges and universities are "outsourcing" many institutional functions to private vendors or other education institutions, including operation of residential dorms, employment training, and even academic functions such as remedial education and beginning language instruction. University hospitals have formed partnerships with both nonprofit and for-profit health organisations. Other institutions have established shared-use facilities with private enterprise.

Consequences of state funding declines

State funding declines and resulting institutional strategies raise the following questions:

Access, success, and diversity

How will further tuition increases affect student access to and success in higher education? Unless sufficient need-based financial aid is provided, low-income students and historically under-represented ethnic groups may be excluded. Even if students and their parents are able and willing to pay higher tuition, some institutions and state policy makers facing fiscal pressures are preparing to cap or even reduce enrolments, despite growing enrolment demands.

Impacts on faculty

Over the next decade, many new faculty will be needed, both to replace the large numbers of expected retirements and to teach the growing numbers of students. How will conflicting forces of budget constraints and the need for new faculty affect how many faculty will be hired and for what types of positions? Although student/faculty ratios could rise—indeed, many faculty positions were eliminated during the recession of the early 2000s, primarily by not replacing tenured faculty and not renewing contracts for non-tenure-track faculty—new faculty will nevertheless be needed. In this environment, both public and private institutions may hire an increasing proportion of faculty who are ineligible for tenure, generally at lower salaries than tenure-track faculty.

Programme reallocations

In a more market-driven environment, will institutions

respond by shifting programme resources toward fields that promise tuition-paying students high-paying jobs or that bring in more external research grants? To date, the impact of budget cuts on programmes appears largely unplanned. In some cases, disproportionate numbers of faculty positions in certain fields have been left vacant, leaving an imbalance between faculty expertise and institutional needs.

In terminating non-tenuretrack faculty, institutions have indirectly made decisions to reduce or eliminate programmes such as remedial education, beginning language courses, and teacher education, which often depend heavily upon non-tenure-track faculty. Repetitive across-the-board cuts have gradually weakened once viable programmes until they become obvious candidates for termination. However, as fiscal constraints continue, more institutions are intentionally reducing, consolidating, or eliminating specific programmes. State policy makers have at times been the driving force behind programme reallocations.

Over the next decade, humanities and social science programmes may be at risk if institutions implement budget systems that require departments to generate income equal to their costs. Or to generate revenues, these departments may increase both enrolments and teaching loads and reduce teaching costs by using more adjunct faculty. If so, this would exacerbate the difference, especially within universities, between a relatively low teaching-load and highly research-oriented science and engineering sector and a relatively high teaching-load and less research-oriented humanities and social sciences sector. If institutions are to prevent such imbalances from growing, they may need to consider reallocating scarce dollars to support important areas unlikely to be sustained by extramural dollars or high tuition. Where programmes are being eliminated, students should be given adequate resources or alternatives to complete their degrees.

Conflicting pressures on governance and control

Within the institution, budget constraints may lead to both greater centralisation and greater decentralisation of authority. Slaughter concluded that retrenchment "generally undermined faculty participation in governance and faculty authority over the direction of the curriculum." At the same time, institutional decisions to require academic units, especially professional schools like business and law, to become self-supporting through tuition revenues or private gifts and contracts tend to shift control from central administration to more autonomous units and to diminish adherence to institution-wide missions. At the state level, many states are demanding greater and more detailed accountability of diminishing state revenues, for example, over faculty workload, even as other states are considering reducing controls in exchange for reduced state appropriations.

Impacts on the higher education system as a whole

Will declining state funding, along with government or market limits on tuition, widen the gaps between the "haves" and the "have-nots" in the higher education system overall – between faculty and student resources at most public institutions and those at well-endowed private institutions, between elite and less elite institutions within the public sector, between tenuretrack and non-tenure-track faculty, or between science and non-science fields? The answer in many cases appears to be "yes."

Over the past decade, the gaps have grown between public and private institutions on a number of measures generally considered quality indicators, such as faculty salaries and student/faculty ratio, leading to questions about whether public institutions can retain past levels of instructional and research quality. This problem may be particularly severe at public two-year or four-year comprehensive institutions, which have fewer opportunities to offset declining state dollars with federal grants or private gifts. Another issue is the distribution of students among institutions. If tuition at public institutions continues to rise, will enrolments shift from public to private higher education or from four-year to less expensive two-year institutions?

In recent years some small shifts in these directions occurred. However, enrolment shifts to public two-year colleges assume that two-year colleges will have the resources to enrol more students and that students can afford their rising fees. If insufficient resources force institutions and students to make choices, non-traditional students, including returning adults and those whose initial preparation precludes admission at other institutions, may well be shut out of traditionally open-door community colleges.

Commercialisation

In the past 25 years, significant changes in the nature of scientific research have occurred. These include the development of fields and techniques not even imagined a quarter century ago, growing university/industry collaboration in the commercial marketing of research discoveries, increased targeting of federal research funding for specific projects, more political involvement in funding – and in prohibiting funding – of research in politically charged areas, and a movement toward "big science" projects involving hundreds of researchers and billions of dollars.

Between 1980 and 2000, industry funding for university research and development (R&D) in science and engineering grew much more rapidly than any other funding source, nearly doubling as a percentage of total university research dollars, from four to almost eight percent. Although this is a small percentage of total dollars, industry support plays a much larger role in certain fields, such as biotechnology and civil engineering. During the 1990s, pharmaceutical funding for university biomedical research shot up. At a time when there are concerns that the growing national deficit together with increased expenditures for federal defence and security may lead to reduced federal research funding, researchers may seek industrial sponsorship much more aggressively.

University/industry partnerships, where researchers in both sectors are jointly involved in research activities, have also grown dramatically over the past two decades. This trend reflects the increasing permeability of boundaries between the two sectors, as universities engage in more commercial marketing and as more new Ph.D.'s take jobs in industry but maintain ties with their former faculty advisers. One indicator of this is the growth in the number of university-based research centres with close ties to industry, which increased nearly two and one-half times between 1980 and 1990. Another indicator is the increasing proportion of articles co-authored by academic and industry researchers in fields such as engineering, as well as physics and clinical medicine. Federal and state agencies have further stimulated these partnerships by linking research funding to industry participation; as a result, even public funding takes on characteristics of industry sponsorship.

University/industry collaboration can provide additional sources of support for university research, access to a broader range of talent, and more rapid development and transfer of useful products like vaccines. However, such collaboration is also subject to potential problems. These include hindering the flow of research information and of graduate students' degree completion when industrial sponsors require researchers to delay release of potentially marketable results; suppressing undesirable results; and skewing research agendas toward corporate interests. Nor are these impacts limited to the hard sciences and engineering.

High-profile cases where corporations have provided millions of dollars to universities in return for prior review of and right to delay presentation or publication of results or for influence in setting the research agenda have raised concerns about bias and inhibition of research, as well as the use of universities' credibility to legitimise industry goals.

A still more problematic trend is the growing involvement of university researchers and of universities themselves in the commercial marketing of scientific and technological discoveries. During the 1980s, leading university researchers established or became associated with for-profit biotechnology and other "high-tech" companies based on their federally funded university research. Many universities have established for-profit technology-transfer units designed to speed the flow of scientific discoveries and products to the private sector and bring dollars to the institution. They have also encouraged spin-off companies based on faculty research and have acquired equity in the spin-off firms they generated. Universities have moved aggressively into securing commercial patents, especially in drug and other biomedical areas, as well as negotiating royalty and licensing arrangements with private companies.

Between 1993 and 2002, the number of patents issued to academic institutions increased almost two and one-half times, although two-thirds of these went to just 13 universities or university systems. These trends reflect the confluence of two developments: a growing eagerness of universities to exploit the economic potential of research activities conducted under their auspices and the readiness of entrepreneurs and companies to recognise and invest in the market potential of this research.

Many of these efforts suffered a setback when the high-tech "bubble" burst in the economic recession at the start of the twenty-first century. Nevertheless, despite strong faculty opposition in some cases as well as the limited success of these initiatives at most universities, they are likely to grow, especially during a period of limited state and federal funding, because they promise universities increased revenues.

Like industry sponsorship, commercial marketing of university research also poses threats to the research system, among them the possibility that it will create conflicts of interest for individuals and institutions, restrict the flow of information, increase the university's fragmentation into entrepreneurial fiefdoms, and shift power to non-academic personnel who typically control for-profit enterprises within the university. Critics also charge that commercialisation may further shift research priorities toward more marketable areas in science and technology fields, distort traditional academic missions, and replace science dedicated to the public good with the "privatisation of knowledge."

Changing Approaches to Higher Education

The governance and coordination of higher education differs enormously by public versus private control, type of institution, and state, and it differs within each of these categories as well. Historically, most higher education institutions had their own governing boards, although their powers and those of different campus constituencies varied widely. While most institutions and almost all private ones still have individual campus governing boards, most students and faculty now study and teach in institutions that are part of multi-campus systems, a few with hundreds of thousands of students. In addition, all but a handful of states have a statewide coordinating or governing board with some degree of authority or responsibility for all public post-secondary institutions in the state and sometimes for the state's private institutions as well. During the 1980s and 1990s, significant and sometimes unpredicted shifts in the powers and structures of governance or coordination at each of these levels - campus, multi-campus, and statewide - occurred. Political and budgetary forces make it likely that additional changes will occur in the next decade.

At the campus level, the past two decades have seen contrary movements toward more centralisation and more decentralisation of authority. College and university presidents and other top administrators have gained more authority to deal with budget pressures and external demands for accountability, and continuing pressures make it likely that this trend will continue. Simultaneously, a number of institutions have decentralised substantial control to individual schools and departments as a means to centre accountability in the units directly responsible for instruction and research, and more institutions are exploring this option. Some units, especially professional schools, have in effect been spun off from the larger university.

Decentralisation and "responsibility-centered budgeting," which rewards entrepreneurship and priority setting, are creating new approaches intended to increase flexibility at lower institutional levels and, in some cases, enable resource reallocation to other institutional functions or units. These approaches, however, also raise questions as to whether university-wide missions and values will be maintained and whether departments that typically have not had the slack that comes with large amounts of external funding will retain their priority. Shared governance between trustees, administration, and faculty is another ongoing campus governance issue. At some institutions, particularly elite universities with long histories of faculty influence, shared governance remains strong. At these institutions, except in extraordinary cases, faculty in departments and through academic senate committees retain authority to make faculty hiring and promotion decisions, select graduate students, determine the curriculum, and with administration set the broad outlines for campus priorities and directions. However, some scholars argue that at many institutions faculty have become "managed professionals." Moreover, shared governance may be undermined in the future as the percentage of faculty who are not permanent increases.

Governance and structures of multi-campus systems are in considerable flux. As with campus governance, there are conflicting trends, and generalisations are difficult because the functions, powers, and integration of these systems vary substantially. In some cases they are loose collections of very different types of institutions. In other cases they are a set of relatively similar campuses with common admissions and faculty promotion standards, under a relatively strong system-wide board and administration. During budget crises, system-wide administrations have often been cut more extensively than those on the campuses.

Depending on their powers and traditions, system-wide governing boards and administrations have the potential to exercise broad leverage over their campuses through budget and programme review powers. Systems may act as buffers against political intervention or as channels for it. On the one hand, system boards and administrations may reduce campus autonomy and flexibility if they impose inappropriately standardised priorities or expectations. Systems also increase bureaucratisation and make shared governance more difficult to achieve. On the other hand, system-wide leaders can bring to bear broader perspectives on the overall educational needs of the campuses and the state. System leadership—boards, administrators and system-wide faculty committees—may be especially important in matters that have relatively weak campus constituencies but are important to the system or to the state, such as undergraduate general education, teacher education, or improvement of school education. They may also ensure that a last surviving programme in a particular field is not eliminated through uncoordinated actions by individual institutions. Especially during tight budget periods or under political pressure, system administrations may provide incentives for intercampus collaborations that individual campuses are unable to mount—for example, for programmes in less studied languages. How well these collaborations survive when budgets improve is uncertain, however. Moreover, where a system office does not exercise adequate quality control, other more political actors, such as the state's executive branch, may step into the vacuum.

FUTURE OUTLOOK

We are going to witness a revolution in the nation's colleges and universities. The following changes stand out.

There will be a greatly expanded and far more diverse set of higher education providers. Today there are thousands of colleges and universities around the world. For the most part, though they are public and private, the vast majority is nonprofit. In the years ahead, they will be joined by for-profit higher education and non-profit knowledge organisations, such as museums and libraries that have entered the post-secondary market. Many corporate universities are far more advanced than traditional colleges in terms of pedagogy, curriculum design, and evaluation. Nonprofit and for-profit foreign universities will also join the fray. We will see competition between for-profits and not-for-profits as well as partnerships between and among sectors.

Some colleges, particularly low-endowment, low-selectivity private schools, will face increasing pressure simply to remain open as competition grows. Institutional closures will rise. New brand names and a new hierarchy of quality in post-secondary institutions should also be an expected consequence. The innovation leaders are far more likely to come from the new providers as well as from those demonstrating the best customer service and the most commitment to assessing programme performance. In this sense, traditional higher education may well become the follower rather than the pacesetter in this new post-secondary world.

There will be three basic types of colleges and universities. One type will be the traditional campus-based university. Let's call these "brick universities." Another type will be the new virtual university. These could be called "click universities." The third version will be a combination of the two, which could be called "brick and click universities." The most successful brick universities are likely to be residential colleges appealing to more traditionally aged students. The exclusively click universities will focus on non-traditional populations. Today's major universities are likely to try to become brick and click institutions that, if current findings on e-commerce are correct, should be both the most competitive and most attractive market in higher education. Although consumers appreciate the convenience, ease, and time-independent nature of shopping online, they also want the physical presence of the store for returning merchandise, getting expert advice, trying on and viewing products, and having interaction with sales people and even other customers. Higher education's for-profit competitors already know this.

There is likely to be an unbundling of the traditional functions of higher education. The functions of higher education are traditionally described as teaching, research, and service. Teaching is the only one of these functions that is universally profitable to colleges and universities. Everyone else loses money. Consequently, the new providers in higher education will only be interested in teaching. They will compete with colleges and universities only in the realm of instruction. Although this is a wise business decision, it raises a big issue for the nation. To the extent that colleges lose out to their new competitors, the offsetting funding for two activities of vital national interest is lost. The policy question that must be addressed is how do we protect the research and service functions? An institution that engages only in research and service is not financially viable, and it may not even be intellectually viable.

Faculty will be independent of colleges and universities. With the rise of virtual universities, the spread of technologies within higher education that enable institutions to reach dramatically larger audiences, and the entrance into higher education of a well-funded for-profit sector, the keys to the future will be the best faculty and the best content.

There will be worldwide campuses. For the most part, colleges and universities are associated with a particular nation. For click universities and click and brick universities, national boundaries have no meaning. The result will be the rise of global universities. Which institutions make the transition will depend on their speed of action and the quality of the products they produce. Global for-profits and schools that already operate around the world have an edge if they can develop the cutting-edge pedagogy for the new Internet technologies that will shape the future.

Higher education will be individualised. Instruction will be available anytime or anyplace. Students will be able to receive their education on a campus, in the office, at home, in the car or on a train, in a hotel, at a conference, or on a vacation. That instruction will occur throughout a lifetime. It may be in multi-year blocks, months, days, or hours. The student will be able to choose the form of pedagogy most consistent with how he or she learns from numerous, different suppliers. The focus of higher education will shift from teaching to learning.

Today higher education focuses on process. In general, students study for defined periods, earn credits for each hour of study, and are awarded a degree upon earning a specified number of credits. With the individualisation of education, the growing diversity of students, and the multiplication of providers, the commonality of process is very likely to be lost. With this change, the emphasis will necessarily shift from standardising process to measuring outcomes. Accordingly, the emphasis will change from focusing on how students are taught to determining how much students have learned.

Degrees will wither in importance. Degrees today are the certification of time spent in a college. From college to college, there is little comparability of common quality or even of content in the studies constituting the same degree. The degree signifies a period of successful college attendance, the class rank suggests the relative degree of success, and the name of the college indicates the quality of the degree.

With the change in emphasis from process to outcomes, degrees become far less meaningful or useful. It would be far more helpful to have a transcript of each student's competencies, what they know and can do. This might be a series of certificates or a statement of each skill or knowledge competency a student achieves. To record student achievements—throughout a lifetime in different settings using varied learning methods in perhaps different geographic areas—it will be necessary to establish a central education recording bureau and provide each person with a portable record of their educational achievements. This record might be called an "educational passport" or a "portfolio."

Educational dollars will follow students more than institutions. Again because of the multiplication of educational providers and the emphasis on outcomes, it is likely to make sense to government and private funders to invest their money in the student rather than institutions. Now funding of public universities by the state is a norm. States may choose to increase competition and reduce both funding demands and dependence on physical plant by redirecting the money to the consumer. This would raise large questions about the independence of higher education and the degree to which colleges and universities will be required to be market-driven and consumer-oriented in the way most for-profit schools are.

4

TECHNOLOGY USE IN HIGHER EDUCATION

Technology is driving the demand for new forms of higher education because the pace of change in the workplace is requiring adults to be constantly retrained. Education, and associated credentials certifying learning, will increasingly be required on an ongoing basis as our workplace evolves with ever-increasing change. Technology will also provide us with alternate forms of postsecondary education delivery that will better meet the ongoing education needs of working adults.

Technology in higher education affords the opportunity to create a learning environment that is learner-centric, individualised, and interactive. Technology will greatly expand access to higher education and fundamentally change the models of education with which we are familiar. In particular, technology will enable education that is learner-centric, individualised, and interactive, making education far more relevant to the needs of individuals. It will allow for anytime, anyplace learning, which will be particularly attractive to working adults, and it will enable true lifelong learning in a formal sense. These new forms of educational delivery will require new ways to measure and credential learning.

Although modern technologies may have a place in helping students visualise real-world phenomena or, through distance delivery, in providing classes that might otherwise be unavailable, they are primarily linear, passive presentations of material in the tradition of classroom instruction. They represent distribution of current models of education, but they offer no new educational paradigm.

Specifically, online education enables us for the first time to put knowledge and learning within reach of all those who have access, at the time and place where such knowledge is needed. Internet-based education offers the potential of thousands of classes on hundreds of subjects available anytime night or day, at any place, at the convenience of the student. Although post-secondary education has been both place-bound and time-bound, we now have the opportunity to truly have anytime, anyplace learning. Although the source of knowledge and learning has traditionally been the professor, knowledge and learning is now available over the Internet.

Teachers in traditional models perform as a "sage on the stage." What new paradigms help create is a "guide on the side" model. These two phrases describe succinctly the difference between teacher-centric classrooms and learner-centric classrooms. In the former, teachers are presumed to be the font of all wisdom and knowledge. Their job is to move that wisdom and knowledge from their own brains to the receiver brains of their students.

Almost nothing is taken into account regarding the personal context, knowledge, or experience that each learner already brings to the learning situation. Students are seen primarily as empty vessels or passive receptacles waiting to be filled. The availability of thousands of classes over the Internet enables learners to select their own learning choices from the offerings of many sites, order them the way they want, and pursue the outcomes that are important to them. This shift to learner-centric education has already begun, and it will take on added momentum as high-quality instructional content becomes available over the Internet. High-quality instructional modules will enable individuals to access the knowledge they need when it is needed, moving to "just-in-time" education rather than "just-in-case" education.

TECHNOLOGY-BASED EDUCATION

The research and service contributions of universities are an important component of our free and innovative society. There is significant evidence that research universities have positive economic effects in their communities. Campus-based universities and colleges also serve as an important "transition point" for young people graduating from high school, who are not yet prepared to enter the workforce and serve as fully participating citizens. The social aspects of the campus experience are important elements of learning at this stage of life, though they receive no credit or grade.

The model of existing universities and colleges is based on the idea that postsecondary education is an opportunity, generally for 18- to 25-year-olds, to dedicate several years to learning and preparation to become fully functioning adults ready to enter the world of work. Technology will impact, to some degree, our traditional campuses and students.

Universities will teach technology use and will have ongoing requirements to have the latest technology available. Professors will increasingly require students to use the Internet for research and supplemental information and sometimes for communication and collaboration. Some universities will develop a "brick-andclick" approach by offering a combination of classroom courses, online courses, and hybrid courses that combine online teaching with classroom discussion, as well as offering online courses through their continuing education departments to reach out to other learners.

However, the use of technology does not change the fundamental distinctions between our traditional educational system and the new models of online learning. Those distinctions are in the role of the student, the role of faculty, and the role of the institution. Most institutions, especially educational institutions, have difficulty in reinventing roles, so it is likely that new institutions will take the leadership role in online learning. The new models of online education serve different functions than our traditional universities. Fundamentally, online education is more applicable to lifelong learning than to education as an event, and it is more applicable to working adults than to students just out of high school.

Student's Role

Online learning implies learner-centric education, where learners take responsibility to choose learning activities of most value and relevance to them. Traditional-aged students (18 to 25) are generally not able to take such responsibility. They do not yet have the experience in work and life to know which learning is most important. Moreover, many of these individuals benefit from the social interactions of a campus.

In contrast, adult learners generally have full-time jobs, families, and a good idea of the additional education they need. They have little patience to sit through long lectures of information that may or may not be relevant. These students are able to take responsibility to define the learning that is important to them, and they will be demanding consumers of educational content. Many of these individuals simply cannot participate in formal education that is place or time specific. They require the anytime, anywhere learning afforded by online education.

Faculty's Role

In traditional institutions, faculty members are perceived as the sources of knowledge, and their role is to communicate that knowledge to their students. With students who have little experience, there is arguably a common body of knowledge that needs to be taught and is relevant for most students. However, in the information age, the amount of knowledge and information is doubling every few years. It is no longer possible for professors to master more than a small slice of the current knowledge in their field.

Research and researchers will continue to be vitally important to our society. Yet, with the increasing amount of content available over the Internet, the challenge for students is not access to information and knowledge. Understanding what is most important to know and where the best source of that knowledge lies are the challenges. Consequently, the role of faculty in online education shifts to mentoring—directing students to appropriate content; helping them learn how to learn and to find, sift, and judge the quality of information; and encouraging their progress.

Role of Institution

Our universities and colleges are set up to define the learning that is required. They do this through required courses, prerequisites, and a specified number of credit hours. They also do this at the course level, with each professor deciding what he or she will teach in a given semester. Institutions certify learning by having professors assign grades to student performance and by counting credit hours completed toward a degree.

Generally, an institution certifies only the learning that is done there, with some provision for the transfer of credits from elsewhere. In online learning, learning experiences may be from anywhere, not only from other universities and colleges but also from personal study or corporate training and work experience. The role of institutions will be to certify learning regardless of where it is done. This will change the institutional role from mandating classes and credit hours to developing measurements of knowledge and skills.

CHALLENGES FOR EFFECTIVE TECHNOLOGY USE

The potential of online learning cannot be realised without addressing some significant challenges.

The quality of instruction is paramount. Many of the current online courses are of very poor quality, amounting to little more than professors putting their lecture notes online. To the extent that courses are simply text-based, electronic correspondence courses, they will be no more effective than those same courses in print form. The two most significant priorities in developing online courses governors can support are that they be modular and interactive.

Modular content enables students to individualise their learning experience by skipping parts that they already know and focusing on modules that are relevant to their individual needs. New online content should be developed as learning objects, each addressing a particular objective, that can be linked to form modules and courses. New standards are being developed for learning objects to make them interchangeable. Effective online content is also highly interactive, utilising the power of the computer to process student responses, provide specific feedback, and modify instructional paths based on student performance.

Developing high-quality online courses is expensive. A typical development team would include, at a minimum, an instructional designer, a subject-matter expert, a graphic artist, a programmer, and an editor. Although faculty members are often the ones tasked with putting courses online, few if any of them have all of these skills. A few universities are organising to support faculty development efforts, but this is not widespread, partly because of the high cost of doing so. The only way for institutions to afford the cost of high-quality course materials is to amortise the cost over many students by sharing courses.

The current model is for every institution to develop its own set of online courses. However, from a national or state perspective, it makes no sense for an institution to be funding another English 101 course if there are already 10 good ones available from other institutions. There is no reason for 10 institutions to each develop a course in a particular subject, if they could pool their expertise, share the costs, and generate one really excellent course for all to use. Although the idea of sharing courses in many ways goes against the tradition of our universities as individual silos of learning where faculty design their own classes, there is a precedent in the use of nationally published textbooks.

The concept of sharing online content, in the form of courses or simply individual learning objects, raises the issue of intellectual property rights. The issue is most often framed as to whether the faculty or the institution owns the course, but the issue is more complex. Developing high-quality online courses is beyond the capability of most faculties. It requires the skills of a team and the corresponding investment, and the challenge is to have adequate incentives for faculty, other team members, and the institution to participate in the development and wide distribution of online courses.

The revenue-sharing model is more important than the ownership question, but both must be addressed to enable the maximum sharing of content. At the same time, if states are funding online course development at state universities and colleges, they should be insisting that these courses be used across the state, and perhaps shared among states, rather than the same courses being developed at each state institution.

The major challenges to distance education during the past 50 years have been low student completion rates and the lack of collaboration one would experience in a campus environment with both faculty and other students. However, Internet-based education can potentially address both of these issues. Collaboration over the Internet, using chat rooms, threaded discussion groups, message boards, and other tools, may be even richer than the interactions on campus.

Increased collaboration leads to a sense of a learning community, and as a result, higher completion rates. The addition of faculty mentors to work with and encourage students has a further positive effect on completion rates. Nevertheless, these elements of e-learning are not present in many models and require thoughtful implementation.

Technologically mediated learning means new roles for students, faculty, and institutions. These new learning models also produce new roles for state policies and new opportunities for governors to harness this powerful tool.

NEW MODELS FOR ASSURING QUALITY

The governments have the opportunity to frequently and compellingly convey the need for new models for assuring quality and credentialing learning.

Post-seondary education has long been self-regulated, through regional accrediting bodies, and more recently, through various national accrediting groups. The departments of education, corporations, government entities, and other universities accept accreditation as a certification of quality education. Accreditation is required for central financial aid, for government and corporate tuition reimbursement, and generally to attract students to institutions of higher education.

Traditionally, accreditation has looked at the quality of institutions and the qualifications of their people and processes. More frequently, quality assurance processes are beginning to assess the quality of learning at an institution. For example, the National Council for the Accreditation of Teacher Education is reforming its quality assurance process to include a demonstration by teacher candidates that they can connect theory to practice and be effective in the classroom. Pass rates on a content knowledge test will be used in the accreditation decision.

Although institutional quality assurance is moving toward recognition of skills and knowledge obtained, technology-based education will enable learning to take place in many ways and many places outside of traditional higher education institutions. If learning is directed by the individual and not by an institution, and if that learning is unique to each individual and may be accomplished either through formal classes, by independent study, through work experiences, or in other ways, then the measuring and credentialing of that learning become critical. Perhaps the most important impact of the Internet on education is that it transfers authority from learning institutions to individuals. This trend, at least for adult learners, will lead to some surprising consequences.

Individualised education will lead to individualised accreditation or certification of learning achieved. This trend is already well underway in the technology field, with industry certifications. This trend will spread to other disciplines. As a result, the role of our education institutions must expand to measure and credential learning regardless of where that learning occurs, or new institutions will be formed to provide this function.

There will be a greatly increased need for, and acceptance of, competency-based certifications rather than traditional grades on transcripts. Historically, universities have held the position that "the only learning that counts is the learning you do here." Learning is measured in credit hours, and the degree of learning is measured by attendance, classwork, assignments, and tests, which are created and assessed by instructors and reflected in grades.

Although this system will continue to be used with traditional campus-based students, it is inappropriate for the new models of online learning. Where learning may have been done anywhere, and in a variety of ways, the measurement of learning will move to measuring outputs—what one knows and can do—rather than activity. Ultimately, there will be a preference for independently determined competency assessments *instead* of grades. This preference is already being expressed by employers and is demonstrated in the technology certifications developed by industry.

In the end, if students can define, obtain, and validate their own learning, and employers find the validation reliable, then the meaning and value of a college degree is redefined. Although accredited universities and colleges largely control access to higher education today because they control the credentialing of learning, the higher education landscape of the future will be more open with different kinds of acceptable credentials and different forms of accreditation and validation of learning.

In addition to calling for new models of assuring quality and credentialing learning, governors can help articulate the need for swifter quality assurance processes. Regional accreditation is typically a five- to seven-year process, which is a huge barrier to entry for new participants in the education market. Even after accreditation, new degrees must be individually approved, which can take three to six months after the degree is developed.

Although appropriate in past societies of limited change, the slow pace of traditional accreditation is not responsive to the New Economy requirements for education. For example, because of changes in technology, many programs of technology instruction have an effective life of only two to three years. Essentially, new programs in postsecondary education must circumvent traditional accreditation, as is the case with the burgeoning demand for technology certifications.

IMPLICATIONS FOR GOVERNMENT POLICIES

Governments and institutions should support online education as an alternative to traditional campus-based education, particularly for working adults, but also for rural students who may be unable to attend a traditional college or university. Online education has the potential to make a significant difference in workforce development and economic competitiveness. To make this happen, the authorities can take the following actions.

— *Ensure that Internet access is widely available.* This includes ensuring access to computers and infrastructure among those who might otherwise not have such access. It also includes giving all individuals the basic knowledge to use the access provided. Knowledge of computers and the Internet is essential in the New Economy, but this knowledge is made exponentially more important because these tools will be key to all kinds of learning.

– *Support financial aid eligibility rules to support study in qualified e-learning programs.* To promote online learning, adminitstrators can advocate for changes in government policies. They can also put e-learning on an equal footing with more traditional classroom education by recommending changes to state financial aid programs and policies that promote online education.

– *Recommend that state and industry tuition reimbursement provisions include e-learning.* States should actively utilise e-learning for the ongoing training and development of state employees. States should also include and even encourage e-learning solutions in their requests for proposals for workforce development programs.

– *Support the development and acceptance of alternative measures for assuring quality education.* Historically, both government and industry have relied on traditional accreditation for assuring quality in education. As a result, only courses from accredited institutions are eligible for tuition reimbursement, accreditation is a requirement for central financial aid, and accreditation is a requirement to bid on many government education and training jobs. Both government and industry need to measure quality by measuring the knowledge and skills acquired by their employees; such measurements will enable new and innovative programs, as well as technologies, to demonstrate their practical worth without a lengthy formal accreditation process. States need new processes to license alternative providers that can demonstrate the effectiveness of their programs, rather than leaving this task to traditional accrediting processes.

– *Shift public post-secondary education funds from institutions to individuals.* While continuing support for existing state universities and colleges, governors should carefully assess the need for more campus buildings in a learning environment that may increasingly be online. Over time, the funding of higher education should shift to financial support of individuals rather than institutions. Money will then flow to educational providers that best meet student needs, encouraging and increasing competition in higher education and empowering students to choose learning experiences that are most relevant to them.

5

ACCOUNTABILITY IN HIGHER EDUCATION

There is little question that for the last several years, providers of higher education have come under increased scrutiny from government agencies, the general public, accrediting bodies and the media, and from more directly involved stakeholders. In the latter category are students, faculty, parents, alumni, the community in which the university is located, and those private individuals and institutions who donate resources. Among the issues which have drawn the attention of these groups and agencies are:

– the value/cost ratio of higher education,
– the expectations of expanded technology and scientific breakthroughs, and
– the paradox of public esteem.

Furthermore, colleges and universities are now counted upon to be environmentally accountable and to monitor their educational performance utilising internal and external audits. In addition, they are expected to show a sense of responsibility by performing outreach and demonstrating a concern for and active participation in the welfare of their local communities. From the standpoint of governmental scrutiny, universities are required to demonstrate diversity, to accept responsibility for such egalitarian measures as affirmative action, and to abide by all federal and state regulations. This occurs in the face of often declining funding support for education by governmental agencies. Private colleges are not immune to calls for greater accountability. With tuitions continually rising, students, parents, and other constituencies are demanding proof that students are getting what they are paying for and learning what they need to know.

Accountability in higher education is not new. It is de ja vu all over again. In the late 1960s, as higher education grew to what was then considered to be unprecedented levels, and as student demonstrations concerning civil rights and other issues erupted throughout the nation, the general public became more skeptical about the role of mass higher education. Concurrently, the value of all social institutions was being questioned, and the government's role in other social concerns expanded. All of these factors, and many more, gave significant impetus to higher education entering an era of accountability. Mention the term "accountability" as applied to higher education and a number of negative images immediately arise.

State legislators see colleges and universities as secretive, over reactive, and quick to label any external imposition an attack on academic freedom and institutional autonomy. Conversely, campuses view public officials as uninformed and unrealistic. State officials are seen as too impulsive about intervening in their eagerness to demonstrate to taxpayers that only their timely intervention can assure quality and contain skyrocketing tuitions. Internally and externally to the academy, concerns are expressed about higher education's departure or deviation from its historic and traditional role and mission—a change in purpose—and the underlying notion that the public's trust is being violated. Despite these sometimes-negative images, accountability does serve important public purposes. It is a public-oriented process that seeks to assure public constituents of the value, effectiveness, and quality of higher education. It not only informs the public about institutional performance, but also is an opportunity for colleges and universities to show institutional commitment to continued progress over time.

CONCEPTS OF ACCOUNTABILITY

Accountability is an obligation or willingness to accept responsibility or to account for one's actions. It imposes six demands on officials or their agents for government or public service organisations, including colleges and universities.

– they must demonstrate that they have used their powers properly.

– they must show that they are working to achieve the mission or priorities set for their office or organisation.

– they must report on their performance, for "power is opaque, accountability is public".

– the two "E" words of public stewardship – efficiency and effectiveness – require accounting "for the resources they use and the outcomes they create".

– they must ensure the quality of the programmes and services produced. Last

– they must show that they serve public needs.

The last five of these accountability demands represent tall tasks for higher education because of its unique purposes, collegial governance, and diverse constituencies.

The term *accountability* raises several deceptively simple but devilishly difficult questions: *Who* is accountable to *whom,* for *what* purposes, for *whose* benefit, by *which* means, and with *what* consequences? The pronouns *who, whom,* and *whose* represent, respectively, the traditional trio of agent, principal, and beneficiary in political and organisational theory. In democracies, elected officers such as governors and legislators are the agents, while the "general public" plays the dual role of both principal (delegating the authority) and beneficiary (receiving the ultimate rewards).

Delegation of authority down the chain of government agencies adds to the confusion about *who* is accountable to *whom.* As delegation and decentralisation drop deeper in government and public service organisations, agent self-interest rises while the sense of public purpose recedes Delegation especially affects the academy, with its prized autonomy and collegial governance. At the state level, higher education coordinating or consolidated governing boards are nearly always the agents exercising the authority delegated by governors and legislators as the principals, mostly over public colleges and universities but, to some extent, over private institutions as well. The beneficiaries are, ultimately, the general public and, more immediately, students, businesses, governments, and social and civic organisations.

At the campus level, senior administrators become the agents, exercising the delegated authority of their principals and boards of trustees for the immediate benefit of students and external clients and, ultimately, for the public at large. Moving down the campus-delegation ladder, professors, in theory, exercise the authority delegated through deans for the same beneficiaries. It is indeed a long distance from the initial delegation of authority from governors and legislators to state higher education boards to the professors providing the instruction, research, and service that benefit society. Not surprisingly, in such long-distance delegation, both the connection and the communication often become unclear.

The concepts of upward, downward, inward, and outward accountability represent types of connections between principals and agents in higher education and other public services.

- *Upward accountability* represents the traditional relationship of a subordinate to a superior. It covers procedural, bureaucratic, legal, or vertical accountability.
- *Downward accountability* focuses on a manager being responsible to subordinates in participatory decision making or *collegial accountability* in higher education.
- *Inward accountability* centers on agents acting on professional or ethical standards and often appears in organisations dominated by professionals, such as in colleges and universities, where it becomes *professional accountability*.
- *Outward accountability* means responding to external clients, stakeholders, supporters, and in a democratic society, ultimately, to the public at large. It includes market and political accountability.

Accountability for what becomes even more confusing and changeable. Clarity is an uncommon characteristic in elected government and collegial governance. Both often sacrifice clarity for closure, if not consensus. In addition, higher education—the knowledge and information institution in a knowledge and information society—suffers from too many, often conflicting expectations. The purposes or goals of accountability programmes for higher education have shifted over time from system efficiency, to educational quality, to organisational productivity, and to external responsiveness to public priorities or market demands. As is often the case in public policy, new purposes are always added, but earlier goals are seldom abandoned.

Academics always argue that the academy is different, and accountability is no exception. Insiders see the differences between higher education and other public services as arising from the special character of the academic profession and its responsibilities. Outsiders counter that discovering and disseminating knowledge is no more complex and challenging than the problems confronting other professions, such as medicine and law. The presence of professionalism in higher education and other specialised organisations does complicate accountability.

Contrary to popular opinion, professors are not the only professionals who make that claim. The correct claim of academics for special treatment relates not to their profession but to the special role of higher education in society. Robert Berdahl vividly describes the dual demands of this unique claim.

Universities have generally had ambivalent relations with their surrounding societies: both involved and withdrawn; both serving and criticising; both needing and being needed. Berdahl and others insist that colleges and universities must stay sufficiently safe from external pressures to safeguard their societal critique yet sufficiently responsive to external needs to sustain societal support. They must simultaneously serve and scrutinise the society that supports them.

These dual roles demand both autonomy and accountability. As is often the case, balance is the key. Too much autonomy encourages colleges and universities, both public and private, to slight society's needs. Too much accountability produces dependent institutions subservient to society's whims. Somehow, higher education and society's representatives must reach for an agreement that seeks the middle ground of service without subservience.

COMPACT BETWEEN HIGHER EDUCATION AND SOCIETY

Society and the academy once appeared to have such an agreement. After World War II, stimulated by the success of the GI Bill, a social compact seemed to exist between American society and higher education. Although bows to state and regional differences are always in order, this compact clearly covered the country. It rested on a few felt but unwritten principles—on trust, not rules. Americans accepted as an unquestioned act of faith that access to a college education was a public good for society, as well as a private good for students.

Access to college opportunities allowed our nation to champion both sides of the American dilemma of how to achieve both equality and quality. Equality meant that society offered the opportunity for college to a growing percentage of the population while leaving the achievement of quality to the talents and efforts of individuals. Americans also acknowledged the need for a surprising degree of academic autonomy from governmental control.

On a more practical plane, the compact obligated state taxpayers to provide adequate operating funding for public colleges and universities, which in turn would keep tuition reasonably low. In addition, states with strong private colleges and universities supported some level of choice for students who wished to attend private or independent institutions. The compact depended on mutual trust that each side would keep its share of the bargain. The federal policy of supporting basic scientific research in universities added research and service to the social compact of public benefits. People who never went to college or directly benefited from research or service saw higher education as a public good.

Like most compacts, the one between society and higher education became strained when rights and responsibilities moved from vague generalities to specific demands and competed for funding with other public services. Specifics always strain consensus, as do funding constraints. In addition, external complaints about the rampant costs, questionable outcomes, inadequate outputs, and the internal focus of colleges and universities raised successive questions about their economy, quality, productivity, and responsiveness to societal needs. Recessions and falling revenues contributed to these complaints. As a result, universities and professors began a long slide from objects of awe to subjects of accountability.

The social compact that provided the glue between the general public and higher education stuck fairly well through the 1950s to the late 1960s, when student lifestyles and war protests alienated some of the general public and government officials. During these decades, the older public and private colleges and universities expanded, and new campuses emerged to meet the burgeoning demand for college education spurred first by the GI Bill that encouraged returning soldiers to enrol in college and then by the so-called baby boom of their sons and daughters. The following decades brought problems that undermined the consensus of the social compact. Although the problems and programmes of accountability never fall neatly into ten-year spans, the decades described next capture the changing trends.

By the early 1970s, fissures in the social compact opened up, beginning with the falling revenues from a recession and fears of enrollment declines at the end of the baby boom. States adopted more centralised governance through coordinating boards and multicampus systems to control development of new institutions and programme duplication. In response to an anticipated decline in enrolment demand, more centralised governance sought to limit the resources granted to higher education. With economy as the goal, regulation became the lever of accountability and bureaucrats the agents. A pattern developed in this first decade of decline in the social compact. Each partner started holding the other side to more specific and stringent tests. States and society reduced support and demanded more services; colleges and universities requested more funding and started raising tuition, although not nearly to the degree as in the next decade.

By the 1980s, external concerns moved from economy to quality. Complaints about the lack of student learning in public schools, eventually moved to college campuses. Two-thirds of the states mandated, by legislation, that public colleges and universities adopt plans for assessing student learning. State officials dictated the policy but left the method of determination to campus professionals. Assessment shifted the focus of accountability from centralised state regulations to decentralised campus processes for identifying the knowledge and skills that graduates should possess, developing the method for assessing the extent of their achievement, and using the results to improve institutional performance. Although assessment programmes focused on campus processes, the real goal was improving quality outcomes in student learning. This approach tried to combine public accountability with professional autonomy by tying external accountability to institutional improvement.

By the late 1980s and especially the early 1990s, the expanded services provided by federal, state, and local governments shifted the emphasis of public accountability in government and public services from procedural protection to performance production. Osborne and Gaebler called for "reinventing government," which focused on organisational results and customer services. Governments, in line with businesses, should decentralise authority while holding unit managers responsible for reaching designated results. Reinventing government combined *decentralisation* with *direction* by being tight on setting goals and evaluating performance but loose in allowing managers to choose the means for achieving the desired results. Decentralisation encouraged "managerial" accountability, while direction on the desired results ensured "political" accountability.

In line with reinventing government, the 1990s continued decentralisation for higher education but this time with definite directions. Programmes in the 1990s dictated the goals of efficiency and effectiveness through indicators measuring institutional performance but generally left campus managers to determine the means of achieving these ends. Aside from the deregulation movement, several factors forced the change. The first two stemmed from the decline in public funding and from what outsiders perceived as the slow response of higher education to the needs of a knowledge and information society. Burgeoning enrolment demand in the South and West as a result of the "baby boom echo" added to the pressure.

State governments and coordinating boards adopted policies of performance reporting, budgeting, and funding. Whereas assessment policies focused on campus processes, performance programmes supposedly centered on outputs and outcomes. State policymakers replaced campus professionals as the agents of the new accountability.

In the first years of the new century, the thrust of accountability seemed to shift again. Reduced state revenues from another recession and competition from rising costs of Medicaid and public schools once more reduced taxpayer funding for colleges and universities. As public support diminished, public demands escalated, confirming that taxpayer support and public demands are seldom in sync.

Increasing student enrolments and exploding state needs in workforce and economic development, as well as in public schools and teacher training, call for increased responsiveness from colleges and universities. Although the rhetoric on a college education as a public good remains in speeches by governors and legislators, students and parents are expected to pay a rising share of the costs through tuition and fees for what is often seen in state capitols as more of a private benefit for graduates. Private markets increasingly drive developments in public as well as private colleges and universities. States leave more and more of the directions and costs of higher education to private markets, while managing them at times, by intervening to encourage public priorities through programme and funding initiatives.

ACCOUNTABILITY CONFLICTS

Although recent decades brought changes in accountability concerns, the conflict continues between "civic" and "collegiate" interests and cultures. Recently, a third interest has arisen: the "commercial" or entrepreneurial culture. To outsiders reflecting civic and commercial interests, campus resistance to public accountability in the name of academic autonomy seems a cloak covering self-interest to protect special privileges. To academics immersed in the collegiate culture, external insistence on accountability often appears as an intrusion on the independence required for critical appraisal of society and government and for the nurturing of the arts and humanities. As usual, the motivations on and off campus toward accountability and autonomy are mixed. The civic and collegiate cultures create a series of accountability conflicts or, at least, tensions.

The following contentions between the cultures build on those presented by Bogue and Hall. All of them represent variations on the single theme of tensions between institutional autonomy and external accountability—internal interest coming first and the external concern second:

– Institutional improvement versus external accountability
– Peer review versus external regulation
– Inputs and processes versus outputs and outcomes
– Reputation versus responsiveness
– Consultation versus evaluation
– Prestige versus performance
– Trust versus evidence
– Qualitative versus quantitative evidence

These contentions represent not only self-interests but also realistic concerns of the academic community and society's representatives. A beginning in the process of reconciliation of societal interest and academic concern is to recognise the validity of each of these elements. Effective accountability systems should address both sides of these dualisms—a tall task in a land that all too often applies the sportlike scoring of "win" or "lose" to policy decisions.

ACCOUNTABILITY MODELS

The past and present models of accountability suggest little progress in the process of reconciliation between the collegiate, civic, and commercial cultures. Higher education has featured at least six models of accountability:

– bureaucratic,
– professional,
– political,
– managerial,
– market, and
– managed market.

Each model has its own levers or drivers, agents or actors, and goals or purposes. The goals have shifted over time from efficiency to quality to productivity and, finally, to responsiveness to public priorities and market demands.

The techniques differ by model. Bureaucrats like rules. Professionals demand consultation. Policy-makers prefer planning, although government officials still revert to regulation. Managers calculate costs and benefits; entrepreneurs respond to customer satisfaction and anticipate market demand. Each approach seems suited to different conditions. The *bureaucratic* model demands stability, the *professional* requires autonomy, and the *political* necessitates consensus or at least majority consent. The *managerial* model works well in dynamic periods of considerable change. Both *market* models adjust capacity to demand, with government incentives shaping supply and demand to suit public priorities in *managed* markets.

Each model has positive or negative consequences based on performance or results. The bureaucratic rewards compliance with continuation and penalises deviations with sanctions. Success in the professional model encourages consultation on decisions; failure results in neglect of professional advice. Financial incentives represent the positive and funding losses the negative in the political model, although performance reporting usually has only a positive or negative effect on the reputations of colleges or universities because it lacks a formal connection to funding. The management approach involves either promotion or demotion, or possibly acclaim or disapproval. Markets produce profits or losses, and managed markets add incentives to the positive consequences.

Bureaucratic accountability centralises governance. All the other models, with the possible exception of the political, demand decentralised decision making, although the political, managerial, and managed markets add varying degrees of policy directions. The political model can lead to intrusive regulations. Some of the accountability models rest on mature theories, but others represent practices outrunning theory. Each accountability model has generated accountability programmes that accent the goals of efficiency, quality, productivity, market responsiveness, and public priorities.

Of course, the accountability systems in place are seldom as pure as the above categories may suggest. Each model has advantages and disadvantages, depending on application and timing. Bureaucratic accountability lives on in many states and constantly threatens a comeback in all organisations, public or private. Recent scandals in the stock market remind us that some regulation is required to prevent outrageous behaviour. Conversely, uniform regulations do not work well in diverse and complex organisations such as colleges or universities. Professional accountability is essential to effective accountability systems in colleges and universities, but it can lead to gridlock in collegial decision making and to diminished responsiveness to public priorities or market needs. Policies and politics, management and markets are necessary parts of accountability in state higher education systems and in public and private colleges and universities. Yet each of these levers can divert higher education from its fundamental purposes in favour of momentary fads.

TOWARDS COMPLETE ACCOUNTABILITY

Declining state funding, strong market pressures, and growing political involvement in state coordination and campus governance are undermining consensus on the public benefit of post-secondary education. State governments and public research universities developed an extraordinary compact.

In return for financial support from taxpayers, universities agreed to keep tuition low and provide access for students from a broad range of economic backgrounds, train graduate and professional students, promote arts and culture, help solve problems in the community, and perform ground-breaking research. Yet over the past 25 years, that agreement has withered, leaving public research institutions in a purgatory of insufficient resources and declining competitiveness.

The strongest threat to higher education autonomy these days comes not from government power, whether state or federal, but from market forces. Market accountability leaves the setting of public priorities to market demands. Its supporters doubt the efficacy of collective planning of programme initiatives and funding decisions and believe that market forces are more efficient and effective in allocating programmes and resources. Others counter that markets reflect private interests of dominant segments of society and not the public interests of society as a whole. A new approach combines public and private interests called *managed market* accountability.

It follows the admonition in reinventing government of "steering" rather then "rowing." Instead of owning and substantially funding organisations of service delivery, governments can shape or "manage" markets by purchasing or subsidising the services they want. This approach allows government to shape higher education's response to market mechanisms to achieve greater efficiency in the use of scarce public resources. Again, balance is the key. Effective accountability systems must include enough market pressure to ensure reaction to external demands and sufficient policy direction to ensure responsiveness to public needs while considering legitimate academic concerns.

The lack of agreement on those public needs—what states and society need most from colleges and universities—agitates the antagonism between academic organisations and external groups. Absent agreements on expectations from higher education, commitments remain open-ended, demands unrestrained, and stakeholders dissatisfied. Governors, legislators, and business leaders continually call for colleges and universities to start new programmes and services while constantly castigating them for trying to be all things to all people. In turn, academics complain about being labelled unresponsive, when government and business leaders are unclear about their priority needs or change them with election or market cycles.

Few forums exist that bring academic and civic and business leaders together in ways that produce mutual understanding. The two groups too often see each other at their worst rather than their best. Governors, legislators, and business leaders see administrators and professors mostly at budget times haggling for more money like other special interests rather than at work delivering relevant programmes in teaching, research, and service. Academics often complain of shortfalls in state and private funding instead of recognising the sizeable support that governments and businesses already supply. The widening gap between stakeholders and academics undermines the one characteristic that all the writers see as essential to the balance between accountability and autonomy—*trust*. Contrary to the cliche, familiarity is more likely to bring appreciation than breed contempt.

Outsiders criticise the lack of accountability in higher education as an inalienable right but accept no responsibility for creating effective accountability systems. The role of critic without commitment has long been popular in civic circles, no less than on college campuses. Behn, in *Rethinking Democratic Accountability*, talks of moving from "360-degree harassment" of government from all sides of society for failing to satisfy their special interests to "360-degree accountability," where civic and business groups accept responsibility with government officials for setting priorities and ensuring their achievement. His approach transforms criticism into commitment. In some states, business, civic, government, and education leaders are beginning to move from 360-degree harassment to 360-degree accountability in higher education.

Higher education has a long list of participants who must become partners in accountability. They include, internally, students, faculty, staff, and trustees and, externally, leaders of schools, governments, business, labour, civic organisations, and electronic and print media—all of which benefit from higher education programmes, activities, and services. Collaborative or 360-degree accountability suggests the truth in the cliche, "If you are not part of the solution, you are part of the problem."

360-degree accountability calls for courageous leaders of colleges and universities. Colleges and universities must *stick* to their missions, *serve* their society, and *sell* their services. Each of these actions in some ways fights with the others. A college or university, public or private, that sticks with its mission may well miss the next market wave. One that "sells" usually tells customers what they want to hear; one that "serves" often sends a needed but unwelcome message.

Indeed, the college or university that serves society best may well be the one that criticises and resists a slavish devotion to market forces, which are often momentary fads. A single campus cannot do everything that markets demand. It should do what it does best or better than others, which means sticking to its mission while selling to clients who need its services most. Finally, the politically savvy leader in higher education is the one who can distinguish public needs from partisan demands and persuade the general public and hopefully government officials to see the difference.

ACCOUNTABILITY TRIANGLE FOR HIGHER EDUCATION

Burton Clark's famous triangle used state control, academic oligarchy, and market model as the three forces dominating coordination of higher education systems in a comparative international context. His governance triangle estimates the influences of these three factors in coordinating national systems of higher education. The figure 1 substitutes state priorities, academic concerns, and market forces to create an Accountability Triangle for higher education. It assesses the responsiveness of accountability programmes to the three interests and pressures that most affect higher education:

1. *state priorities* reflect the public needs and desires for higher education programmes and services, often as expressed by state officials but also by civic leaders outside government;

2. *academic concerns* involve the issues and interests of the academic community, particularly professors and administrators;
3. *market forces* cover the customer needs and demands of students, parents, and businesses, as well as other clients of colleges and universities.

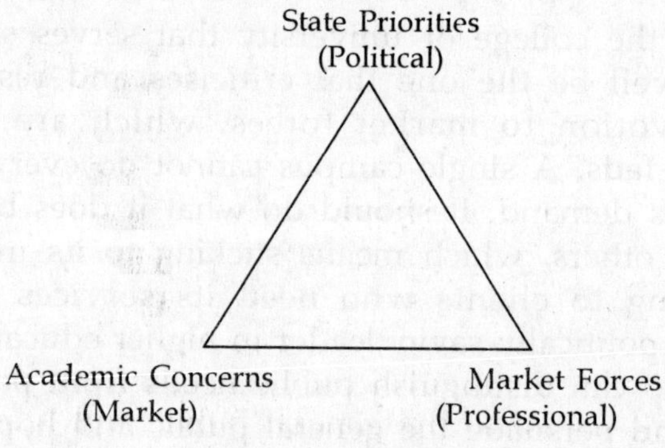

Figure 1. Accountability triangle

State priorities, academic concerns, and market forces also reflect, respectively, the civic, collegiate, and commercial cultures and interests. State priorities represent political accountability, academic concerns reflect professional accountability, and market forces push market accountability.

Each of the three corners of the Accountability Triangle has a bright and a dark side, reflecting both broad needs and special interests. State priorities can constitute what the citizens of a state need most from higher education, such as better schoolteachers, an educated workforce, and an informed citizenry. It can also replicate the partisan interest of the party in power. Academic concerns can encourage free inquiry and discussion of ideas, beliefs, and institutions infused by openness, scholarship, and objectivity. It can also reflect the resource-reputation model of higher education that views institutional quality as mostly a matter of recruiting the brightest students, hiring the faculty stars, and raising the most resources. Market forces can mean meeting the real needs of citizens and society for programmes and services or responding to the dominant economic interest in a state or to commercial schemes or consumer fads.

By and large, state priorities, academic concerns, and market forces present conflicting demands, with some interesting exceptions. At times, the drive for prestige and reputation merges academic concerns, public priorities, and market forces and succumbs to the wiles of the resource-reputation model of excellence for colleges and universities. This odd coupling produces more lawyers and physicians than society needs rather than the nurses and teachers that society requires.

At times, the demand for research in an economy driven by innovation unites the interests of state priorities, academic concerns, and market forces. State priorities and market forces have some common interests, but the former calls for public priorities, whereas the latter relies on private preferences. In addition, state priorities should last longer than market forces. Higher education and its colleges and universities, both public and private, are inevitably accountable to state priorities, academic concerns, and market forces. They should serve all while submitting to none of these imperatives. Being accountable to each of the three corners of the Accountability Triangle means balancing the response to ensure service without subservience to public priorities, academic concerns, and market forces.

Given the importance of state priorities, academic concerns, and market forces as representing political, professional, and market accountability, the centre of the Accountability Triangle seems the ideal spot for an effective accountability system and perhaps for some of the accountability programmes.

AUTONOMY AND ACCOUNTABILITY

Accountability pressures on institutions of higher education have been driven in recent years from a variety of sources and stakeholders. These "drivers" include the concerns of policy makers, elected leaders, and educational leaders about higher education's role and responsibilities, quality and performance, and its perceived rising costs.

UNESCO's 1998 Statement from its World Conference on Higher Education included the following:

> "*The academic* freedoms of higher education institutions and their wide autonomy—which have to be strengthened and protected—are essential if these institutions are to carry out their mission. Autonomy presupposes accountability to society. Institutional autonomy and academic freedoms are necessary for the effective functioning of the higher education system, for the strengthening of its capacity to change and anticipate, for the carrying out of its watchtower or observatory functions, for the assertion of its moral authority in the debate on the great ethical problems and the major issues of global significance, but also for its development as a place where democracy can be practised and promoted. It must be added that the academic freedoms which, in a way, serve as a justification and basis for the critical function of higher education presuppose the observance of certain principles and norms, while laying upon higher education institutions the duty of objectivity, impartiality and intellectual rigor."

While the autonomy granted to an institution of higher education was significant at the time of its origins, and probably up through the 1960s, it has less meaning today as governors, legislatures, and finance departments have developed "the power of the purse" in sophisticated ways.

The need to safeguard and recognise the important value and principle of academic freedom in the classroom and in research and scholarly writing argues strongly for substantial autonomy of higher education. Yet, amidst increasing calls for accountability, the states and higher education must seek a balance between autonomy and accountability. Absent the achievement of balance, higher education will find itself dealing with the increased efforts undertaken by external bodies and political interests, including intrusive behaviour, micro-management, and bureaucratic substitution for professional judgment.

Additionally, policy makers—particularly elected officials—are an important component of a state's accountability system as they, too, are to be held accountable for their role, or lack thereof, in ensuring that there is effective and clear public policy in place, accompanied by fiscal support for the state's goals and objectives through its higher education enterprise. Absent such a component in a state system of accountability for higher education, the state is seen as neglecting its role and responsibility. However, autonomy in higher education with respect to the state is, in the contemporary setting, only part of the total picture of institutional freedom. Higher education is increasingly subject to pressures from sources other than the state: market forces, competition for students and staff, and the commercial interests in commissioned research. For good and bad, such a trend will reduce the traditional values of the state higher education relationship, yet public trust will continue to be an important issue to be addressed by both parties—the state and higher education.

If a contemporary but balanced accountability regime is to be developed, more trust must be built and sustained among the key players: faculty, institutional administrations, governing and coordinating boards, elected policymakers, state budget officials, the media, and ultimately the public. Such a balance can only be achieved where there is leadership, vision, and trust among and between the important players in the state and its institutions of higher education. This balance will require clarity, understanding, and foresight. It also will require embracing the past, navigating the present, and understanding the future.

Without transcending current boundaries—through collaboration and cooperation embedded in a process of communication, and by reaching across the extended state and higher education enterprise through a process that is unifying in its intent—there will continue to be a diminution of support and trust in higher education and the elected officials entrusted to represent the public interest.

In recent years, discussions about accountability for higher education have become both common and contentious. Many reasons for this have been advanced, but virtually all can be related to two factors: declining public resources and the sense that colleges and universities are ill-prepared to meet the needs of the 21st century. Policy leaders at both the state and federal levels have struggled to improve higher education's responsiveness to these conditions through a range of increasingly proactive initiatives. But they have experienced growing frustration about the inability of their actions to change the ways colleges and universities behave.

A new political climate also has emerged emphasising deregulation and government down-sizing. Both conditions have decisively shaped the way policymakers approach conversations about accountability. Struggling hard to make ends meet, institutional leaders meanwhile are in growing rebellion against what they perceive as overly bureaucratic approaches to achieving accountability. At the most basic level, they see complex, overlapping, and duplicative systems of reporting and assessment that are unnecessarily expensive in terms of time and resources.

In addition, they view with alarm a growing shift away from established institution-centered measures, such as accreditation, and toward government-mandated, standards-driven accountability systems they believe threaten institutional diversity and autonomy. Protecting these perceived historic virtues of higher education is the principal agenda they bring to the accountability table.

Amidst the calls for accountability there continue to be voices raised relating to the historic recognition of autonomy and institutional independence. Concerns focus attention on the mounting intrusiveness, intervention, and micromanagement of states in the affairs of its institutions of higher education, whether by statute or through the power of the budget. And, at the national level, there are mounting concerns about efforts to overhaul the higher education data collection system to include what is referred to as a "unit record" system whereby each institution would submit records on individual students, including such details as Social Security number, gender, ethnicity, data of birth, tuition, loans, grant awards, permanent and local addresses, number of courses, and number of credit hours.

Central to the condition of the higher education sector in this nation is its social contract—a need to have political and social legitimacy—and the respect and confidence of the people that it serves and their elected representative bodies. The roots of such a relationship are typically historic, yet have stood the test of time. Such a relationship is referred to as *the public trust*. In his comparative perspective on accreditation processes and their fundamental links to higher education, Martin Trow articulates what the *public trust* is and why it is an integral component of an effective higher education system, and an accountable one:

> [One] of the fundamental links between higher education and society is trust—that is, the provision of support, by either public or private bodies, without the requirement that the institution either provide specific goods and services in return for that support, or account specifically and in detail for the use of those funds....Trust is also the central element in the very significant contributions by private organisations and individuals to American colleges and universities both public and private, for which no accountability is demanded. Trust, indeed, is the basis of the very large measure of autonomy of colleges and universities anywhere which are able to raise substantial sums of private money, or which are funded by governments which voluntarily delegate much of their power over the institutions, and thus give to the institutions a large measure of autonomy in the use of the funds they provide.

With considerable authority and autonomy granted by statute or a state's constitution, and absent a strong regulatory or coordinating agency or centralised college or university system, colleges and universities must assure elected officials—as representatives of the public—that they are responsible stewards of the public's money and can deliver quality education at an affordable price. In essence, they must demonstrate that they are accountable, responsible, and trustworthy. In all states, including California, autonomy and accountability are interrelated.

A search for balance between autonomy and accountability is important as the nature of accountability is undergoing a change, particularly as it relates to where it is and where it is going. Equally important is the relationship between accreditation and accountability. Peter Ewell—who is an informed and insightful observer of higher education and public policy as well as being utilised by many states and institutions of higher education to provide advice and counsel on policies involving accountability, accreditation, and quality assurance—believes the fact that the nature of accreditation's first purpose—"accountability"—has been experiencing a fundamental redefinition that will radically challenge the kinds of public assurances of institutional quality that accrediting organisations will be called upon to make. "Put simply," according to Ewell, "this redefinition changes the definition of accountability from adequate processes to publicly acceptable performance and results."

Among the trends contained in the emerging view of accountability are these three main ingredients.

- *Performance*. The first and most notable aspect of this evolving conception of institutional accountability is how overwhelmingly it is centered on results. This convergence mirrors a decade of transition in the notion of quality assurance—reflected in other arenas ranging from business to medicine—from inputs and processes to absolute performance as the critical marker of accountability. Accreditation has gradually accommodated this view of the centrality of institutional performance, and most regions now similarly reflect this trend in their growing emphasis on providing evidence of student learning outcomes in accreditation reviews.
- *Transparency*. A second important dimension of this emerging concept of accountability is its emphasis on openness and public disclosure. But the notion of transparency as an emerging element of accountability goes well beyond simply making the results of periodic reviews more accessible. Taken in its emerging spirit, it implies that an institution of integrity will be most accountable when it

conducts its most important business openly, so that its key stakeholders can see how it routinely operates. Considerable accountability to stakeholders is in this way achieved because the institution's assets and actions can be readily "audited" by anybody at any time, simply because it does so much of its most important collective business in a spirit of openness and inclusion.

– *Culture of Evidence*. A final dimension of the emerging notion of accountability is more difficult to describe, as it combines qualities of institutional responsiveness and organisational self-awareness. It is what some refer to as a "culture of evidence" – the disposition of the institution to consider evidence routinely at all levels when planning and contemplating action. From this perspective, an institution demonstrates accountability when it holds itself unremittingly responsible for learning about itself and for using the resulting knowledge to continuously improve its operations in the light of its mission and the needs of its stakeholders.

From the above discussions, it is clear that, it is important for higher education institutions and the states in which they reside to place the consideration of an accountability system within the context of what is needed in the state in terms of its vision for the future. An accountability system for the sake of having one rings hollow, unless it is within the framework of addressing how the higher education enterprise is addressing issues requiring short- and long-range attention, such as:

– ensuring that accessibility to effective, quality colleges and universities is being realised at affordable prices and costs.

– increasing the effective and efficient use of resources.

– identifying student achievement and outcomes, linkages between secondary and higher education, and financial resources and expenditures.

– developing and strengthening an independent coordinating, research, and policy entity as an agency able to bring focus to the issues and direct some portion of the state allocation to higher education towards achieving the kinds of changes identified.

– monitoring and ensuring that more individuals are acquiring the basic knowledge and skills that will prepare them for meaningful participation in some form of education beyond high school.

– providing a focus in the state's universities on increasing highly competitive research, technology transfer, and graduate education, especially in areas critical to state's future economy.

– creating an exciting, vibrant, and relevant higher education system to serve the public and those that take advantage of the higher learning as thoughtful people, as participants in the economy, and as citizens.

– overcoming the organisation of higher education into large, autonomous, and vertically structured universities and systems, which creates significant barriers to efficient coordination, sharing of resources, and coordinated collaboration, in order to meet regional education needs and contribute to economic development initiatives.

6

ACCESS AND EQUITY IN HIGHER EDUCATION

Higher education faces significant challenges throughout the world. Among the most universal and complex are those related to ensuring equitable access for the rapidly growing number of individuals seeking education at the post-secondary level. Meeting the burgeoning demand for higher education and developing policies and resources that provide the benefit of higher education to diverse populations of students will require national commitment and international cooperation. In today's global, knowledge-based economy, the economic growth and social well being of nations around the world are increasingly dependent on a well-educated workforce and individual access to quality education. Understanding the principal components of this challenge and the relationship between cultural norms, social and political policies and the development of higher education will require deeper understanding in order to realise the goals to expand access and equity.

CONCEPTS OF ACCESS AND EQUITY

For the purposes of this chapter, the global, inclusive term of 'equity', used alike for students and staff, refers to

(1) policies and procedures for enabling and encouraging groups in society at present under-represented as students in higher education institutions and programmes or study areas, to gain access to and demonstrate successful performance in higher education, and transition to the labour market and (2) extending opportunities for suitably qualified people, regardless of gender, ethnicity, disability or other extraneous considerations, to achieve staff positions in higher education and to advance professionally according to merit and achievement and without discrimination based on these extraneous considerations.

Terms such as 'access', 'equal opportunity', 'equality of outcomes', 'affirmative action', and 'equity' are frequently encountered in the area of higher education policy and analysis. The key umbrella or organising concept, however, is 'equity' conceived as: fairness; equality of treatment where comparable features and conditions pertain; and opportunity to participate and contribute, without hindrance through prejudice and discriminatory customary practice. Equity in this sense, need not connote equality in any precise or mathematical sense, e.g. fixed quotas for under-represented groups proportional to overall population, lotteries for admission to popular courses or institutions, etc, although as strategies these may sometimes be attempted. Nor does it imply uniformity whether of institutional provision or entry and study requirements. On the contrary, it is now widely accepted that, rather than sameness, substantial diversity and fitness to individuals and groups, and their circumstances, are appropriate if the varied needs of students are to be met. The notion of "fitness" has its roots in Platonic and Aristotelian ideas which give prominence to ideas of distinctive differences requiring individual treatment or the recognition of categories of people for which collective action is appropriate. They have always been relevant in educational provision.

Historically, in educational practice, these ideas have at times been associated with exclusion and privileged access and treatment rather than a fair chance for all. By contrast, contemporary liberal democratic and ethical theories support different ideas about 'fitness', 'fairness' and 'justice'. Most notable, perhaps, are those developed by John Rawls in his theory of justice and, in different ways, by a considerable body of philosophers, social theorists and economists, and resoundingly expressed in the Universal Declaration of Human Rights and the European Convention on Human Rights. Considerateness and concern for the well-being of all people feature strongly in modern intellectual theories and declarations.

The crucial point behind the Declaration and the Convention on Human Rights and by this body of theoretical literature is that equity is put at the centre of discourse and policy: everyone in the community should be given equal consideration and the opportunity to develop human capabilities. Inequality, for example, according to Rawls' 'Difference Principle', in access to primary goods, is acceptable only when it can be conclusively shown that ultimately it gives rise to greater benefits for everyone. More precisely, inequalities above a (low) threshold can be tolerated only when they function to help more people move across it. This of course does not preclude forms of inequality reflecting 'special conditions' and there is considerable debate about the implications of these conditioning factors. Sen, for example, prefers the concept of freedom for all to achieve, or capability.

Despite the differences it is clear that system-wide policies, structures and institutions and their procedures can be expected to submit to the claims of justice, fairness and equal opportunity. Discussion of these concepts and reflective analysis of their educational implications would seem to be an important role for staff and students in higher education.

In modern political analysis, equity is often subsumed under the concept of democratisation – the recognition that all individuals have rights and needs, that these considerations require and have a central role in policies and action strategies. Through participative procedures, whereby all have a voice and an impact, more general concepts are translated into practical action. Decisions should not be pre-emptive, by one group on behalf of another, but should be shared, giving rise to a sense both of individual freedom and of a community of interests and values.

Universities in several countries rather sharply experienced the impact of democratic ideas following the radical student movements of the late 1960's. They are now embedded in national policy frameworks and institutions' decision-making procedures, as well as more generally in such international conventions as those of the United Nations.

In higher education the challenge now is both to fully embrace the concept of equity and with determination to integrate it with the long-established traditions of excellence and merit and the more recent policy preoccupations with standards, quality, efficiency and relevance to social and economic needs. The need for this reconciliation is implicit in the legislative requirements that have been set in Ireland in recent years and in policy proposals designed to strengthen higher education and its role in national development.

Policy must take account of such considerations as quality and suitability of qualifications for specific study programmes, economic and socio-cultural needs, human capital needs, financial and other considerations. Practical issues include the systems of assessment and certification at secondary school level, procedures for managing alternative entry routes which include non-formal learning methods for determining specific qualities for particular higher education programmes. In this regard, OECD countries, until relatively recently, could be classified into 'supply-driven' (e.g. the highly competitive selection procedures in the UK and Irish universities); demand driven (e.g. Italy, Germany, Belgium, The Netherlands) and student market driven, whereby government leaves access to market forces (U.S.). Admission procedures for students fall broadly into one of two approaches, or some combination of them: system-wide right of entry to all who are deemed qualified; institutional selection according to determinations made for particular programmes and courses. For either approach variations can be and often are made under special entry schemes for under-represented groups, for example though the ways points for entry are allocated for specially targeted groups.

In practice, across the OECD membership there are now strong and reasonably consistent moves towards opening up access opportunities for tertiary education to ever wider and more diverse groups. More precisely, 'equity' refers comprehensively to policies, procedures, strategies and everyday actions designed to improve the higher educational, employment and advancement opportunities for those of low socio-economic status, women and girls, ethnic and other minorities, the people with a disability and others denied previous opportunity to enter higher education or discriminated against in various ways. The wish to study and the aptitude to succeed are determining factors but it cannot be assumed that there is some definite standard or level which acts as a threshold. The notion of some fixed quantum of talent, a 'pool of ability', is no longer acceptable. On the other hand, it would scarcely be equitable to offer particular kinds and levels of study opportunities in the certain knowledge that potential students would be quite unable to meet the requirements. Procedures are needed to ensure every opportunity, from early childhood onwards for students to demonstrate their aptitudes and interests rather than depending on the selection role of upper secondary education. Also required are second chance opportunities, especially for mature age students.

'Educational opportunity' refers to circumstances affecting selection and entry to programmes; conditions of study which include curricula, teaching procedures, learning resources and financial considerations; criteria for successful performance and graduation and conditions governing assessed performance; and factors affecting entry into the work force over which higher education has some control or influence.

There is of course a distinction between access for students and equal employment opportunities for staff; nevertheless they can be viewed as part of a single 'equity continuum'. Of particular relevance for present purposes, is employment in academic institutions: opportunities for under-represented groups and those actively discriminated against not only to freely enter the academic labour market but to be promoted fairly and to advance to positions of responsibility and influence.

'Equity' in its broadest sense would refer to all stunts and staff or prospective students and staff – that opportunity and provision should be such as to sustain and advance the interests of everyone. However, such an interpretation, important as it is for overall policy making, would embrace all aspects of higher education whereas the focus here is, as indicated, on particular categories of potential and actual students and staff, traditionally and still often typically under-represented in universities and other tertiary institutions.

'Equity', thus defined, forms a significant element in the extension into many aspects of higher education of notions of justice and fairness and liberal democratic ideas, policies and practices. Although often associated with particular political movements and campaigns the range of issues arising for broad-based equity policies in education goes well beyond the concerns and actions of particular special interest groups.

Great advances have been made over several decades in advancing equity in higher education, for both students and staff. For the 1981 OECD Conference on Policies for Higher Education in the 1980's, access to higher education was one of the four main themes. In many countries, in the fields of equal opportunity employment and anti-discrimination, there are now well-established legislative frameworks and often also a commission and/ or other agencies responsible for implementing legislation, monitoring and reporting on compliance and handling complaints and disputes. Their scope normally includes education at all levels.

Specifically in higher education, and throughout the OECD region, there is a continuing movement to advance equity through these and other means. Unquestionably there has been very considerable progress, through the substantial quantitative growth of university places that has occurred during the past three to four decades.

No less important has been the establishment of a greater diversity of institutions and programmes, facilities and arrangements to meet the needs of individuals and groups previously given scant attention. Success has been achieved in improving access and study opportunities for disabled students; women have made substantial career advances; and universities generally are much better able –and willing – than in the past to construct and implement broad-based equity policies. Increasing participation rates at all levels are one indicator of progress in achieving equity objectives.

DRIVING FORCES OF EQUITY AGENDA

In addition to and partly as a result of the impact of education democratisation movements, and the pressure of special interest groups extending over several decades, the current equity agenda may be said to derive from five main sources:

– determination by governments, public agencies and a variety of policy makers and Non–Governmental Organisations and community action groups to advance the needs and interests of specific categories of under-representation, both students and staff;

– a large and cumulative body of legislation particularly relating to human rights, equal employment opportunities and anti-discrimination, leading to many innovative organisational practices in institutions;

– a growing volume of research evidence on, amongst other things, the limited effectiveness or slow results of many of the legislative and policy measures that have been taken;

– sensitivity of policy makers, system managers and institutions to reports of persistent inequity, and breaches of legislation conventions, regulations, etc.;

– continued representations by special interest groups.

Progress of a substantial kind cannot be gainsaid. These gains have, however, served to identify shortcomings and highlight further needs. The more widespread the experience of upper secondary and tertiary education becomes, the greater the likelihood that those who do not acquire qualifications risk being socially and economically marginalised.

Equity Shortcomings

The fundamental goals of the human rights movement, and policies formulated in many countries for improved access to higher education for under-represented groups and greater equity in academic employment, have not been fully or in many instances even adequately achieved or implemented. Strong evidence for this has been provided in the Council of Europe international study which has recently resulted in a firm and comprehensive Ministerial Recommendation.

For many researchers and commentators, there are genuine grounds for concern, indicating amongst other things weak policies, inadequate implementation procedures and the ignoring of legislative requirements and agreed procedures. Although not possible to quantify in all respects, these weaknesses are sufficiently widespread and well documented as to be the target of continuing criticism and agitation. Even so, there is still a view that the concern in the sphere of education is exaggerated, that there is insufficient recognition of substantial gains already made, too much special pleading and not enough attention to the basic requirements of upholding standards in academic life, of the tradition of excellence.

Some members of minority groups, 'some women' may have had fewer past opportunities. But these are transitional and marginal problems that can be handled within the academic tradition". Unfortunately, the transition is proving to be a very extended one and it is precisely aspects of 'the academic tradition' as embedded in customary practice and institutional structures that have been held up by many researchers and scholars as a cause of continuing difficulty in achieving equity objective. Academia, as perceived by critics, is characterised as traditionally elitist, male and patriarchal in its culture, values and structures. Men, it is claimed, are encouraged by their professors, women not. The valued tradition of collegial decision-making, it has been claimed, can actually inhibit equity, causing senior administrators to hold back from enforcement.

The barriers in the eyes of some critics, are compounded by other factors than gender: "Academia, too, has a class structure: its hierarchy of professors, assistant professors, and part-timers is not solely a ladder based on merit, but a track based on a number of gender, racial/ethnic, and socio-economic factors. The degradation many working-class women experience in academia replicates that of the larger classed society".

The striking image of the 'glass ceiling' has been adopted by women's groups to explain why it is that for some people in higher education there is no great problem in career progression, whereas for others there is a continuing sense of injustice. For men, looking down, there is nothing to see; but women, striving to go forward find themselves hard up against the glass ceiling. There were several reported instances of the strength of tacit resistance to the implementation of equity policies; reports from national equal opportunity commissions also provide many examples of breaches of regulations and laws.

There are conflicting perceptions and points of view. On the one hand, the belief that while there may be problems, procedures are in hand to manage them and, on the other, that there are barriers still to shatter, changes to be made in the academic system itself. There are also questions to raise about categorisation. 'Social class' for example must be defined with reference not merely to patterns of income distribution and their traditional occupational correlates, but to the changing composition of society and indeed to the role of education as itself a nominator of social class. Comparisons over time of rates of participation may not be of like with like.

The issues are complex and warrant careful elucidation. The desire to open up admission procedures must be tempered by a realistic appraisal of student capabilities and the readiness and capacity of institutions to provide suitable study environments. Very high dropout rates in some European countries where access is open are scarcely equity-positive. It is arguable, of course, that still the most effective 'strategy' for achieving equity objectives is expansion, the wave effect that carries all before it. Certainly expansion has broadened opportunities, but these opportunities for higher education are still unequally distributed, even on the strictest interpretation of the traditional merit principle.

Indeed a large part of the rationale for a major international study, by the Council of Europe, is precisely "a concern that this expansion has not fully met the hope placed in it for greater equity between all potential students and for the inclusion of those belonging to social groups historically disadvantaged in respect of access to education". The Council of Europe and other sources do not confine the concerns about exclusion to certain social groups. In access to higher education institutions, lower socio-economic groups, however defined, are indeed under-represented; but women, too, having succeeded in gaining access as students and progressing well, including employment in academic institutions, have not had the success they seek and expect in climbing the career ladder.

Since women are now enrolling in many academic subjects at higher levels than men, the need is for women to accept the challenge of "stepping out of the shadows to take over leadership responsibilities, and believe in their future". These are not the only unfulfilled goals. There are significant barriers facing various categories of students with a disability; some ethnic minorities are very poorly represented either as students or staff; financing arrangements often confer unequal benefits or impose hardships in inequitable ways; and higher education – universities in particular – still tends to advance those already more socially, culturally and economically favoured. Prejudice and discrimination are reported in relation to sexual orientation; adolescent boys are an emerging equity category not yet fully recognised, and so on. These are generalisations, they have different force, impact and significance across and within different societies but they present a generally valid picture of unequal representation and participation across a wide spectrum of countries.

The challenge is real, but policy responses are not straightforward. There are cultural and social norms at stake, political interests and active pressure groups at work pursuing diverse ends. To be equitable, education policies and practices need to satisfy a very wide and varied set of criteria and they require to be negotiated, tradeoffs included. Moreover, they are not, of course, the only relevant criteria.

Higher education must satisfy scholarly standards of excellence or quality, be financially sound and accountable, connect with major developmental needs in the economy and society, meet a variety of community and family expectations, contribute positively to the advancement of knowledge and the education of the professions, and so on. What is not at issue, however, is the obligation, both legal and moral, that increasingly falls upon higher education institutions to demonstrate that equity features prominently and consistently in their stated policies and their practical actions.

Significant progress, like the increase in women's participation in undergraduate education which now, in a number of countries, exceeds men's, is welcomed as is the steady increase in women's employment in academic positions once the exclusive preserve of males. But such changes have not been sufficient for policy makers and many members of the academic community who seek more evidence of progress in achieving goals.

Not only have explicit goals and targets not been met (or even set) in several areas, but the concept of equity has often been defined too narrowly. An obvious example is the widespread acceptance of the principle of applying the same access rules to everyone. This, on the face of it, seems equitable, but in practice it has not assisted in improving access for some poorly represented groups. Awareness of this led to what has been criticised in a Council of Europe study as a 'symbolic model of equal opportunity'.

In this model, while limited numbers of students from under-represented or 'non-traditional' groups have been admitted under special arrangements, the basic fabric of the rules of admission remains intact. What is perhaps more important, it is now recognised that the special arrangements, commendable in themselves, need to be part of a much broader strategy which treats 'access' as but one step or stage in a policy process that should start in the early years of schooling, since it is schooling that, unless reformed, reinforces unequal opportunity. Where interpretation does not extend quite as far as this, it does embrace considerably more than 'entry' or 'participation'.

In the Council of Europe project on Access to Higher Education in Europe, access was defined as:

- greater participation in higher education of good quality;

- the extension of participation to include currently under-represented groups;
- a recognition that participation extends beyond entry to successful completion.

There is a growing realisation that further critical analysis and more substantial measures including closer monitoring and detailed reporting are required to achieve equity goals for both students and staff. In the area of disability, there is, as a result of persistent effort, a much better understanding than in the past of the often subtle barriers that stand in the way.

Regarding women's employment in universities, several decades of experience with programmes of equal employment opportunity have resulted in a much deeper understanding than hitherto of the cultural and organisational boundaries or barriers, that may militate against employment equity, reinforcing discriminatory practices and beliefs. 'Equity' needs to be further elaborated, its frame of reference extended, from specific procedures relating to fair practice in employment or study opportunities, to include the fundamental norms, values, ethos and way of life of academic institutions. Such extension can be quite problematic and is often contested, covertly if not explicitly.

From time to time, governments are alerted to the need for rather more strenuous measures than have flowed from equal opportunity legislation, or they are urged to take a more forceful approach to developing the implications of legislation and giving greater impetus to equity goals in higher education. As the Council of Europe recognised, the legislative approach is itself an important step in advancing equity in higher education, but not sufficient.

Financial obstacles can of course be a considerable barrier, even in regimes where tuition fees are low or non-existent. Costs for supporting non-traditional students, for example, are often high both for institutions and the individuals and these can be critical when they reinforce other socio-economic factors. Tuition fees, even in schemes which are specifically designed to greatly alleviate hardship, may have a negative, discriminatory impact on enrolments. Targeted initiative schemes can be highly beneficial at the tertiary level, particularly in support of labour market policies, but their equity significance may be in question and is in any case lessened if incentives and support for study from an early age are insufficient.

A single institution will be responsible for only part of what might be termed a generic or developmental strategy for equity in higher education, and individual public agencies and government departments will have only partial policy responsibility. Nevertheless, there is an accumulating body of research findings and experiential evidence that supports the need for a more systemic approach in which the roles and responsibilities of various elements and agencies are brought together, into more coherent, co-ordinated policy initiatives.

BARRIERS OF ACCESS TO HIGHER EDUCATION

Despite the many improvements that have been made and the wide range of policy instruments that have been deployed, there remains a formidable array of barriers. They are summarised below.

Barriers to Student Access and Progression

- Characteristics of primary and secondary schooling which favour academic advancement of some groups of students but not others; high dropout and failure rates at secondary school level; lack of transparency in educational provision, of guidance and orientation, and of suitable ways of recording, acknowledging and enhancing achievement and progression for students with learning difficulties or 'school resistance';

- Socio-economic - financial and cultural factors in family and community; growing income disparities and 'poverty pools'; unequal cultural capital across social groups; inadequate forms of liaison and communication;
- Geographic factors that militate against knowledge of availability of programmes and ready participation in them;
- Financial constraints on family and prospective/ actual students; inadequate incentives to continue studying;
- Difficulties facing public authorities and institutions in meeting additional costs for equity purposes in era of declining per capita budgets;
- Legislative gaps; weak policy approaches including procedures for monitoring, evaluation and follow-up; inadequate research-based knowledge of 'what works';
- Rigid application of merit principle and one-sided pursuit of narrow concept of excellence in education including particularist concepts of 'the idea of a university';
- Weaknesses in teacher preparation, supervision and professional development;
- Amongst staff in higher education, a continuing prejudice towards, lack of understanding and willingness or ability to provide support for, the study needs of particular disadvantaged groups;

- Community hostility to consequences of affirmative action, e.g. quotas, heavy subsidies;
- Poor data on performance and inadequate procedures for identifying 'at risk'students;
- Bafflement over/ lack of clear research findings about and understanding of why policy measures have not worked, notably in seeking to improve the ratio of low socio-economic groups in upper secondary and higher education.

Barriers to Staff Recruitment and Career Advancement

- Cultural assumptions, values, institutional structures and procedures favouring traditional patterns of staff recruitment and advancement;
- Lack of knowledge by potential and actual staff of opportunities for careers in higher education;
- Over zealous and confrontationist prosecution of affirmative action programmes;
- Lack of or failure by individuals from under-represented groups to participate in support structures, networks etc. that assist in developing knowledge of opportunities, self esteem and confidence.
- Difficulties, especially for women, of multiple socio-cultural-personal role expectations and requirements;
- Tacit or explicit discrimination against candidates with a disability, members of particular ethnic and minority groups, etc;
- Weak or non-existent policies, structures and procedures designed to overcome inequities in all aspects of staffing at the institutional level;

- Inadequate system-wide policy frameworks including inadequacies in incentives and sanctions;
- Lack of institutional policies and procedures focused on career advancement.

Barriers to Staff and Student Advancement

- Displacement or dilution of the equity agenda by other policy preoccupations e.g. quality benchmarking, economic performance, globalisation and internationalism;
- Deja-vu: a sense that much having been achieved, equity issues are being over-emphasised;
- Ignorance, lack of information about both deficiencies in the present situation and opportunities for improvement;
- Macro-features or changes in society which militate against the pursuit of equity as a major objective. A most interesting example, in some central and east European countries, is the association of equity in the minds of politicians and in society more generally, with the now discredited communist ideology;
- Financial difficulties and resource allocation procedures.

EQUITY TARGET GROUPS

This section addresses the five main equity groups which have been the subject of considerable attention in the policy arena and research literature in many countries in recent decades: low socio-economic status; women and girls; mature age and part-time students; ethnic and other minority groups; persons with a disability. These are not the only under-represented groups in higher education, nor the only groups subject to discrimination in society – for example members of the gay and lesbian communities, members of rural and isolated communities. Also, relevant equity categories may well shift over time as targets for some groups are achieved or nearly so, and as new categories become relevant. A further point is that it is not uncommon for individuals to belong to two or more equity categories at the same time, thus compounding disadvantage.

Low Socio-economic Status

Socio-economic factors affecting educational access and progression have been a policy preoccupation in OECD member countries for decades. In the concern over educational equity arising from the international democratisation movements of the 1960's, there were several strands. In the post war period, and into the 1970's, a major concern was the under-representation of low socio-economic groups in higher education. The economic rebuilding of Europe under the Marshall Plan extended to embrace social reconstruction, with a prominent role for policies aimed at reducing inequality of opportunity. In the USA, there was a revival of the 1920's and 1930's movements to redress social and economic deprivation, strongly reinforced by the Civil Rights movement of the 1960's.

Rates of attrition from formal schooling and low standards of attainment in secondary school examinations have been the subject of decades of research, advocacy and policy initiatives. What must be borne in mind, however, is that while there was a common concern over under-representation of low socioeconomic groups across OECD countries, there were significant variations according to local circumstances.

In Belgium, for example, economically and socially disadvantaged students were the target of policy initiatives, but, equally, so were girls. In practice, regional disparities were marked and this, as in some other countries, led to regionalisation of institutional provision with an emphasis on first cycle (short) programmes. Region and socio-economic status in this instance were to an extent overlapping categories. Despite multiple policies in Flanders, including financial support, the less well-off groups have continued to be (relatively) disadvantaged. Much of the critical literature has been directed at schools' response to socio-cultural factors influencing student performance, and the class bias of schooling.

Both national governments and international bodies in the immediate post World War decades gave a prominent place to socio-economic factors in policy making and analysis. While this has continued, the oil shocks of the 1970's, recession and then the international drive towards liberalisation of markets, the rapid development of new communication and information technologies, economic globalisation and persistent high unemployment levels especially among youth have given rise to other policy preoccupations. The educational agenda has become very crowded, public funding is subject to heavy constraints and the needs of those whom opportunity appeared to pass by have come into competition with many other concerns.

These considerations on the one hand, and the deeply embedded, complex structural factors in society on the other must largely explain the apparent inability of countries to make significant progress in increasing the proportion of people from low socio-economic groups in higher education. However, the issue is not as straightforward as it might seem at first glance. First, it would be a mistake to assume that the category 'low socio-economic' is static, as already mentioned. Note should also be taken of the hopeful trend of inter-generational changes in relative incomes – a function of increased participation rates in upper secondary and higher education. A second, related point is that, while the proportion of students from the lowest socio-economic categories are not in general improving, the overall numbers are, as a consequence of the great increase in numbers of students enrolled. Third, there is need for considerable caution in interpreting figures – not all countries or institutions record socio-economic status and those that do use different definitions and procedures.

In most countries inequalities feature in relations between socio-economic groups. Despite continuing economic support to underprivileged groups, the development towards equal access is believed to be stagnating. This has more to do with 'cultural capital' than with 'economy in a narrow sense'.

Increasing participation is a necessary consequence of realising the stated aim of 'achieving equality of opportunity for access to all forms of education Schooling can serve both as a conduit and a barrier: increasing enrolment rates and diversified routes provide a conduit but, at the same time, can act as a barrier for some families and students.

The differentiated secondary school system is seen to present a series of four thresholds for students gaining access to higher education in Germany: the first is the transition from a common primary school to one of three secondary school systems, only one of which *(Gymnasium)* provides a standard route to higher education. Transitions within the secondary school and qualifications for higher education further whittle down the pool of students whose qualifications will enable them to enter higher education.

In the international research literature, socio-economic conditions affecting student access to higher education have been a strong concern for several decades, greater in some countries than others, muted at times, but persistent. Research and policy measures have centred on: the disparity of opportunity among social classes, with a recurring emphasis on low socio-economic status family background, the concept of cultural as well as economic capital, rural areas and economically disadvantaged regions or areas, and the interactions among these factors. Sometimes, attention has focused on the 'second chance' principle, i.e. increasing opportunities for mature age students but this is quite variable across national higher education systems. But, access once gained, not all problems are solved.

A series of studies of the East and Central European socialist countries conducted by Dutch researchers documents the intergenerational transmission of inequalities – a counterbalance to the argument already referred to, that participation in higher education can effect a shift in the social balance. The Dutch studies have been carried out in the conceptual framework of 'New Class' theories which aim to show how political resources (party membership) displace traditional resource distribution (owners vs non-owners).

The socio-economic issue is fundamental since it goes to the heart of basic aspirations of the democratic society and the role of education in advancing the interests of all people. But its significance is all the greater in that often clustered around social class are issues to do with disparities between rural and urban areas, ethnic and minority discrimination, inadequate housing, health problems, family difficulties and others.

Expansion and diversification have indeed increased numbers in all socio-economic categories but overall the balance remains much the same even in those countries that have tried very hard, through government intervention, to create a more equal society. The very quest for greater social equality may now be in jeopardy as income differentials increase. A question inevitably arises, therefore, about the credibility and effectiveness of measures taken in many countries and sometimes over several decades in the educational drive for equity in social class terms. Powerful forces in the wider socio-economic setting must be more directly addressed if educational policies are to have the desired effect. What is true of education seems to be true also of other 'welfare'fields including health and social services, that resources made available to the underprivileged are also taken up by the middle classes, leaving the relativities unaffected.

Single issue policies, like direct measures to improve access to higher education are clearly insufficient, although they remain necessary. If, as often declared, the educational objective has been to change the balance, to achieve greater equality of access across the spectrum of socio-economic classes, as distinct from a numerical increase as part of a general wave of expansion, the overall conclusion is that the policies have either failed or had only a quite marginal impact.

Women and Girls

Following hard on the heels of the 1960's movement to extend access to low socio-economic groups, although with historical roots reaching back to the nineteenth century, was the drive to increase opportunities for women and girls. From the 1960's onwards and with growing momentum internationally, is a very wellinformed perception that women have been discriminated against in many different ways in higher education as in society at large. The feminist movement has played a key role in developing broad community awareness of these issues but for policy makers perhaps of greater direct interest have been, on the one hand, the legislative changes over a wide array of equity issues, including employment discrimination, and, on the other, a by now substantial body of research and interpretative literature on all aspects of women's participation in higher education, from conditions affecting undergraduate entry to the occupancy of senior administrative and academic management positions in universities.

First are the students, where amongst OECD countries, gender difference in educational attainment varies markedly by generation. Differences between men and women are much more pronounced among older age groups—for example, the proportion of women with only primary or lower secondary education is much greater amongst 55-64 year old women than among 25-34 year old women. There is, however, no significant difference between the proportion of men and the proportion of women in the present generation graduating from the secondary schools of OECD countries.

There have been similarly dramatic changes in gender ratios in tertiary access. In ten out of thirteen OECD countries, women are the majority of first-time university level entrants. High upper-secondary school completion rates, particularly from general streams, which are more likely to lead to tertiary education, are seen to have stimulated this growth in women's access. Many countries report that more than 50% of students enrolling in higher education are female, some as high as 60%. There are, however, variations.

Significant gender differences across the OECD membership exist in the programmes studied at university, with women more likely to enrol in fields related to the health professions, education and the social and behavioural sciences, and less in the natural sciences and industrial and engineering fields. By contrast, in some Arab countries, e.g. Libya, women are in a majority in engineering courses – but fail to gain appropriate professional employment on graduation. Time series data for the years 1990 – 1996, for each of the five OECD countries in which such data are collected, indicate that there has been an increase in the enrolment of women in first degree tertiary education programmes in each of the sciences, engineering and business. But there is still a long way to go.

Concerning graduation, among those OECD countries providing relevant data, more women than men achieve university level qualifications in the humanities and medical sciences; fewer in mathematics, computer science, engineering and architecture; and about the same in law, business and the natural sciences. Engineering and architecture are also uncommon areas for women at the non-university tertiary level.

Attention amongst policy makers has now shifted to what women study, and the level at which they study. This can be regarded as an indicator of the success of what might be termed first stage policies, aimed at increasing female access both numerically and proportionately. Gender differences tend to be higher in advanced tertiary programmes, with men forming the majority among those enrolled in second or higher degree programmes in four out of five countries.

In Flanders, there is an imbalance between, civil engineering and other technological fields (male dominated) and language and general medicine (females). At the doctoral level, in common with other countries, males tend to predominate. The key, according to the Flemish authorities, is choice of study programme in secondary education and even lower down in the primary and pre-school systems, where stereotyping in school, family and community continue, often in subtle ways. Women have tended to be broadly concentrated in lower status studies and not at higher degree level. Recent policy has focused on encouraging women into 'non-traditional' studies.

Such policies can be influenced not only by equity considerations but by labour market demands for specialised expertise which may not be adequately met under a laissez-faire approach. In the opinion of many commentators, firm target-setting needs to be set in a context of free choice: "all students, irrespective of gender [should] have a choice of field of study in higher education, which is only limited by ability and inclinations, and not stereotyped views and institutional constraints."

The official French *government policy is clear:* Article 14 of the law on guidance says that any student who has a *baccalaureat* has the right to a higher education place, in the course of his/ her choice. This policy in practice is affected by opportunities at the *bac* stage—which have been greatly widened - and the ability and readiness of institutions to meet student demand for specific programmes of their choice. The relationship between 'free choice' and 'equity targets' is not straightforward and policies increasingly seek to 'shepherd' women into traditional male courses of study.

Some countries are much more interventionist than others in this regard. By 1997, earlier Australian targets of 40% female enrollment in agriculture, architecture, business/economics and science, and 15% in engineering had been largely met, and federal authorities suggested universities proceed to set specific targets, such as—within science—more females into computer science. Once women have gained access to non-traditional areas, their success and retention rates are high.

Over the 1990s, Australian women's participation in higher degrees—both by coursework and by research—has risen significantly, and is close to parity with men. There have been many changes in fee liability during the past decade, and some of the gains made could be jeopardised by future changes unless the equity implications are kept to the fore. Finance is perceived as a barrier to women's participation in high fee courses, in the context where many women are, as workers or parents or both, returning to study.

In the U.S.A., a country with a great variety and very large scale of provision of higher education, satisfaction with the increases in women's enrollment is warranted, but in a recent study attention is drawn to the reality of the (often uncomfortable) actual situations in which women find themselves as they embark upon or return to study. Major concern has focused on gender balance in university staff, ranging over such issues as occupational segregation including the interplay between gender and ethnicity, the incidence of casualised, low level posts, the role of senior members of the (academic) profession in judging the intellectual output of aspirants and thereby careers. Women academics have an important role to perform in developing women students' *'notions of identity and autonomy'*, but this is not easily accomplished when, as employees, they are predominantly in low status, low paid, temporary, part-time jobs.

In Finland, and typically in many countries, despite women having been in a slight majority among university graduates since 1970, a 1996 study reported that almost 90% of professorial chairs were occupied by men. Only 2 out of 21 rectors were women in the mid 1990s. In the view of the researchers, Kivinen and Rinne, 'together with the policy aiming at gender equality, the expansion of education has served to prolong and broaden women's educational paths, even though they have not always kept their promises in terms of status, pay or positions in the hierarchies of power'. By contrast with the debates over levels of participation especially by lower socio-economic groups and to some extent ethnic minorities and the disabled, the question of women's advancement has been addressed in policy moves as much for the sake of women's post study/academic careers as for their enrolment and participation in courses leading to qualifications. The explanation for this may lie in the relatively rapid erection in many countries of a substantial and complex legal apparatus supporting equal employment opportunities. However, the apparatus itself reflects deeper social, cultural and economic change.

Although the laws, regulations etc, usually apply to all areas of possible discrimination: ethnicity, socio-economic status, religion, age and so on, and in all areas of employment, the women's movement , has organised itself to achieve changes in ways that no other group seems to have managed. This, at least, is the impression given in the literature, of which a large volume is devoted to research, analysis, advocacy and practical examples of steps being taken to achieve women's equity objectives in academic careers.

There is a definite sense of campaigns to be waged and victories won, in this literature. The more equitable representation of women is being sought in different ways and by different means: one Irish group has recently summarised this as "either by confrontation or by consultative collaboration towards a change agenda". Behind these – and other – strategies is a growing body of research evidence on the status of women in the academic, technological and administrative career lines in higher education. There are, moreover, the by now numerous posts and offices of equal employment opportunity that have been established in institutions and organisations, and the meetings, conferences, publications and pressure politics through which the case for equal employment opportunity is being advanced. Information and its publication, whether research-based or more anecdotal, features more strongly in the issue of womens' participation than with any other under-represented group.

The research findings often demonstrate a slow rate of progress, and analysts searches ever deeper into cultural and structural factors within academic institutions that militate against full achievement of the goals and targets that are being pursued. In a study drawing on the Carnegie Foundation's International Survey of the Academic Professions, Poole et al painted a picture similar to that in much of the within-country literature on academic women. Academic work is gendered: although academia sees itself as having a fundamentally meritocratic and collegial ethos, where rewards follow scholarly performance, the academic labour market is segregated and sex-stereo-typed. The work undertaken by men and women academics is similar if not identical in content and working conditions and patterns have much in common. But there are important differences—in self perception, in the way roles are performed, in motivation and above all in certain subject areas in the nature of women's under-representation—and over-representation and in the hierarchical pecking order. Women may be present in significant numbers in universities and other higher education institutions, but they are disproportionately represented in more junior posts and in temporary or contract and part-time positions.

Kogan et al in an OECD study, observed that, in most countries, women occupy less than 15% of academic positions. The number of female university teachers in Germany does not reach 5% of the total although almost half of the students are women. In only a few countries, and only recently, does the figure of women academics rise to 25 or 30% and then it is uneven across subject field. Ruijs, in a study of eight European countries and Turkey, pointed to the rarity of women in senior administrative positions, although there were variations across countries.

In a number of most carefully detailed and documented studies of women in academic life, Burton has explored the impact of equal employment and anti-discrimination legislation, identifying what she considers to be intransigent factors in institutional culture and organisations. In her view, the locus of concern has shifted -and needs to shift further—from formal compliance with equal employment opportunity laws and regulations 'to the degree to which the underlying spirit of the legislation has taken hold institutionally'. Neither the mere passage of time, nor the pipeline effect of increasing female enrolment in degrees would, in her view, remove the structural and institutional impediments to women's access to and advancement in employment in higher education. Women, for example, are disproportionately represented in positions more vulnerable to funding cuts, are poorly represented on key decision-making committees and suffer from prevailing 'habits of thought'. In her view, as in that of a number of other commentators it is ready identification with the spirit of legislation and equity goals that is lacking. The issue is the pervasiveness of the masculinity of organisational cultures or, in the words of Dudovitz "learning how to survive in a basically hostile environment", or "there is no second sex in academe. There is only one sex: male".

Such strongly worded views, characteristic of the feminist movement's determined entry into higher education from the 1960's to the 1980's, continue to be expressed, although in some recent studies writers have distanced themselves from overtly political feminism and have focused both on micro-analysis of organisational and cultural features that they find inhibiting to the advance of women in academic careers, and on the efforts women's groups are making to overcome them. Burton, with associates, has undertaken fine-grained analyses of the equity reports that all Australian public universities are required to make as part of annual negotiations with the Commonweatlh Government for purposes of funding against agreed performance targets. One of her perhaps unexpected conclusions, is echoed in other studies, *"Collegiality tends to recreate the status quo"*.

Less collegiality or rather modified versions of it, and more managerialism are called for even if, in other respects, managerialist models are criticised for asserting corporative values and sharpening hierarchical divisions. Similarly, the increased devolution of responsibility to departments and faculties, combined with the traditions of internal autonomy at the subject level within the institution has not, in Burton's view, led to department heads and deans being held sufficiently accountable for employment equity.

These points raise more general questions about the nature of academic structures, management and decision-making and the assumptions and attitudes underlying them. Equity concerns are caught up in other aspects of institutional life, thus indicating a need to consider a balance of interests and values in forming and implementing interventionist policies.

Mature Age and Part-time Students

The University of the Third Age, for example, active in Japan, France and other countries, provides significant (if under-researched) opportunities for mature age students who, because not enrolled in formal, assessable courses are usually uncounted even though they may be studying within higher education institutions and using their facilities. Statistics do not always take account of what may be large volume enrollment in professional enhancement programmes which universities increasingly conduct in partnership with industry, government departments and professional bodies; data on private providers are often lacking. More and better data collection and evaluative research are badly needed if mature age participation in higher education or access to its facilities is to be well understood.

There is a spread between countries of the so-called 'traditional' entry age because of variations in length of secondary schooling and the practice of 'stop-out' between school and university or college. This is very evident in the Scandinavian countries, for example where a combination of age of completion of secondary education, deferred entry and prolonged periods of study, punctuated by 'stop-out', means that it is common for adults to be in their late 20s or older before completion of initial tertiary qualifications.

Mature age entry, however, usually refers not to these circumstances but to those where, after a prolonged absence from the formal education system, students embark as adults on tertiary level studies, often through special entry schemes, with access and bridging courses, recognition of work experience and so on. The prevalence in many continental European countries of extensive vocational education and apprenticeships has been seen as reducing the perceived need to enrol in formal tertiary-level studies at a later date, as mature age students. Current policies fostering lifelong learning are likely, however, to modify such perceptions.

Well developed special admissions schemes for mature students exist, for example in the United Kingdom and Australia. These countries, along with Japan, Netherlands, New Zealand, Germany and others.

have open university programmes oriented towards older students. New Zealand has a long-standing 'open admissions' route for adults.

Although data are limited, the movement towards life-long learning, strongly encouraged by the international education organisations is, on the one hand, producing better statistics and, on the other, a great deal of renewed policy interest in adult learners. Despite the limited and often misleading data on international trends in mature age participation in some form of higher education, adult education literature indicates some directions which raise questions about equity. Increased provision for mature age students does not of itself provide extra places for the socially and economically disadvantaged. The issue of advantages accruing to those who already have a high level of education is being recognised by policy makers. Additional measures targeted at specific equity groups are needed.

Successful completion of formal schooling is a key consideration in extending opportunity for mature age learning. For those with a sound initial education, there is clearly a role for undergraduate higher education to play as part of its commitment to the lifelong learning movement. On the other hand, mature age entry to study is often supported on the principle of providing a second chance, for those who did not complete secondary schooling, to undertake tertiary studies.

Perhaps the most significant development in the 'second chance' area is the work of open or distance education providers. These include well known open universities in the U.K., U.S.A., Australia, Canada, New Zealand, Netherlands, South Africa, not to mention large scale Asian providers in Thailand, India, Japan, China, and professional networks like the Norway-based International Council for Distance Education and those fostered by the Canada-based Commonwealth of Learning.

Provision of better access opportunities must be matched by appropriate study conditions. Institutions with a strong mature age profile report the need for systematic help in enabling students – especially those from less privileged backgrounds – in learning how to study at the tertiary level. Dropout rates tend to be higher, there is need for access and sub-degree programmes, guidance and tutorial support and specialist staff. Articulation of courses across levels, procedures for credit recognition and course transfer and other flexible arrangements have slowly emerged but tend to be patchy – a weak link in the chain of educational opportunity for adults. The physical location of facilities is not to be overlooked: higher participation rates of mature age students in rural areas, for example, reflect patterns of campus provision or lack thereof.

Mature age students are often part-timers, combining study with employment, family responsibilities and other commitments in the community. Success and completion rates tend to be lower although they vary with type and level of programmes. Consider the profile of a student, who, while not typical, is a real presence in tertiary institutions in many countries: female, living in a small rural town, in low or moderately paid employment, with family and domestic responsibilities, an early school leaver, and now a mature age student by distance education. Study in such circumstances is difficult and challenging; progress is likely to be slow and interrupted.

In countries with very low rates of mature age participation in higher education, there are significant equity issues to address. Indeed, even where rates are relatively high, there is concern that the equity objective of 'second chance' is not being achieved and that insufficient efforts are being made to provide the flexible arrangements and supportive conditions that would increase enrolments and improve success rates. The ambitious lifelong learning policies many countries have adopted cannot be expected to succeed unless the needs of mature age, part-time students are better and more comprehensively attended to. There are large numbers of adults for whom improved opportunities—and incentives – for embarking on pathways leading to and through higher education are needed.

Ethnic and Minority Groups

The fourth of the broadly defined categories of the under-represented, excluded or discriminated against is that of ethnic and other minorities that have endured substantial discrimination. Although different conditions obtain for each of three identified minority groups, resulting in different requirements in equity policies and strategies, a common element is that they are in some measure aliens in or alienated from mainstream culture (even if this is their choice). This is reflected, at least in the Indigenous and Minority groups, in extremely low levels of participation in stages of formal education beyond minimum legal requirements.

Historically, minority groups have frequently not simply been excluded - or have excluded themselves - from higher education but have been actively persecuted, denied basic human rights. Race hate, harassment and discrimination in society at large are all-too-common, creating conditions which militate against tertiary education participation and success. These circumstances provide a spur to mainstream policy makers to take highly affirmative action to try to counterbalance not only the legacy of discrimination but also its continuing expression in present day society.

Although not belonging to any of the above three Minority groups, special mention may be made of the Afro-American population in the United States. Historically exploited over centuries and enslaved, the deprivations suffered by Afro-Americans were a prime source of dissent, leading to a wide repertoire of equity measures in the 1960s in the USA. These have had an impact in many policy initiatives around the world. The American Civil Rights Movement was highly generative, not only in advancing the cause of Afro-Americans and broadening the democratic base of American higher education, but in giving momentum and direction to several dimensions of equitable education. Although the broader goals of that movement have not yet been fully realised, there has been a move forward, from more global concerns to highly specific programmes focused on particular target groups – such as under-representation in science, mathematics and engineering, the provision of pre-tertiary enrichment courses, and the enhancement of the work of the historically Black colleges.

While it is not possible at present to get reliable and comprehensive international statistics on ethnic representation in tertiary education, many countries report that particular ethnic minorities are seriously under-represented at the tertiary level. Very often, this represents a compound disadvantage with, for example, low SES, a rural or isolated or a poor urban location, and weak mastery of the language of tertiary teaching, where the ethnic group speaks a different language.

Because ethnic political arithmetic has often been unjust and explosive alike during this century, collecting ethnic data is necessarily a delicate – and potentially hazardous – undertaking in modern democracies. Privacy laws may make it impossible and 'ethnicity' is differently defined and categorized in different countries. While ethnicity is an overriding element in the personal identity of some individuals, for others it rates as relatively incidental to their overall self-perception. For this last group, the growth of politicisation of ethnicity poses a certain dilemma, and, as with disability, individuals may – whether for fear of discrimination or for privacy concerns – prefer not to identify publicly as belonging to particular ethnic groups. Indigenous groups may also reject the official view of them as 'ethnic' or 'disadvantaged', claiming recognition as 'sovereign peoples'.

Ethnic or cultural under-representation can be a potent force for change in the wider society. In Belgium in the 1960's the Flemish community was under-represented in the university compared with the French community and this was a factor in institutional regionalisation drives: ultimately they formed part of a wider movement towards Flemish autonomy.

Improved educational access and opportunity are signally important steps towards creating greater social justice and social solidarity, not only in multi-ethnic and migrant societies. There is a recognised need for a wider range of innovatory, well-targeted and community linked programmes and activities at both school and tertiary education levels to meet the specific and varying needs of minorities, including those who have been largely 'socially invisible' until quite recently.

Disabled Students

Although still under-represented, the past decade has seen a marked increase in participation in higher education by students with a disability. A significant factor in at least some countries, is seen to be a flow-on from earlier integration or 'mainstreaming' policies at school level, whereby greater numbers of students with a disability are completing secondary schooling and aspiring to university education as a 'normal' continuation. This is a specific instance of the more general situation whereby tertiary education is modifying its practices as a consequence of flow on from primary and secondary levels, as well as experiencing the impact of legislative changes and changing social norms. A further encouragement to tertiary study has been better provision in many countries of financial support and special facilities and equipment for students with a disability. There is considerable variation in the way in which disability is defined in different countries, and no international standard, as such, exists.

The Americans with Disabilities Act 1990, and the Disability Discrimination Act 1992 in Australia both define disability very broadly to include physical, intellectual, psychiatric, sensory, neurological and learning disabilities. While severe mental disability does, of course, preclude some individuals from being potential higher education students, the intellectual capacity of those with other disabilities mirrors that within the population as a whole. Thus, with appropriate support and conditions for study, a good success rate can be expected from those students with a disability who qualify for university entry.

Disability can strike at any time: for some, disabilities have existed since birth (cerebral palsy, some blind and deaf people); for others, disabilities result from accident in childhood or adulthood (blindness, deafness); for yet others, disabling conditions or illnesses develop with age (psychiatric conditions, cancer). Some conditions are constantly disabling (paraplegia, amputation); others can become disabling from time to time (asthma, allergies, multiple sclerosis); others are temporarily disabling (broken limbs). Also, not all disabling conditions are 'visible' (some medical conditions). Disability is increasingly coming to be understood as a condition of life, which may affect many, if not most, during their lifespan.

Two important features distinguish students with a disability from other equity groups. The first is that disability can affect individuals from families throughout the social structure, and at any time with a certain randomness; second, the 'disabled', by and large, are not a tightly knit or easily identifiable group. Only the deaf appear to have developed a p a rticular identity and culture, centred on their common use of sign language. A key difficulty for universities, is knowing how many 'disabled' students there are.

Some countries enable but do not obligate students to register their disability on enrolment forms. Students need to register their disability only if and when they request assistance from the institution with their course (such as special facilities, or additional time at exams). There are various reasons why students with a disability would choose not to register. For example, with the general move towards more accessible university environments in many countries, students may find their special needs are already met.

Other reasons for not registering can relate to fear of discrimination, and privacy concerns. Fear of public disclosure of a disability is seen as a particular problem for staff in a time of retrenchments—particularly when it concerns an 'invisible' medical condition, such as multiple sclerosis. Privacy issues, it may be said in passing, are not only of importance for the disabled: categorization by ethnicity, social class or sexual orientation is not always acceptable and may be illegal. Statistics and definitions in this category and area are therefore to be treated with considerable caution.

Providing the support necessary for students with a disability can be a considerable cost for institutions, although in percentage terms it is likely to be a very small part of the overall budget. Costs must nevertheless be met, and two lines of thinking have emerged: first whether certain higher education institutions should be specially designated and funded to cater for the needs of this group; and second, whether there should be mainstreaming.

In the USA and Australia, the answer is clear – all higher education institutions are bound by anti-discrimination legislation to provide support for any academically qualified student with a disability enrolling in any institution. In some countries, particular institutions have emerged with concentrations of disabled students. The Open University in Britain, as with equivalent institutions in other countries, has proved particularly attractive to disabled students, many of whom tend to be older than other students, and frequently study part-time, or take slightly longer to complete their courses.

Developments in technology have made tremendous differences to the independence with which certain categories of disabled students can pursue their studies. For many students with a disability, educational support can be simple and straightforward with relatively little cost attached (allowing longer time in exams, allowing alternative formats for assignments, provision of learning materials in different formats).

Universities must also think beyond physical and educational/ pedagogical accessibility, increasingly to social accessibility, to enable students to participate in the full life of the institution (e.g. student union outings providing appropriate transport). Isolation is a common experience of students with a disability in higher education, and social inclusion, not surprisingly, is linked with success in studies. These considerations call for an imaginative approach for part-time and distance education students with a disability, including a readiness to liaise with families and local support networks.

Two key challenges in making these changes in universities are, first, to develop a positive attitude towards students with a disability among both staff and the broader student population and, second, for staff to develop knowledge and understanding of the needs of students with a disability and how to make appropriate accommodations for them. As in all equity domains, systematic attention to attitude formation, information and knowledge, and positive institutional leadership are crucial. Ignorance and prejudice regarding disabilities are reportedly still rife in many institutions.

The legal requirements for higher education institutions with regard to provision for disabled students varies considerably between countries. Both the United States and Australia have specific legislation on disability discrimination which places requirements on higher education institutions. In the United Kingdom, higher education institutions are not bound by the disability legislation, but there is a move for them to follow it in a voluntary fashion. In Canada, disability discrimination is covered within a broad human rights legislation. Increasingly there is a move in Europe towards recommendations and regulations concerning persons with a disability. The European Union, OECD and UNESCO have all sponsored activities during the 1990's focused on students with a disability in higher education

Enduring Problems of Access and Equity

For the deep-seated problems, difficulties and barriers that are proving quite obdurate, special efforts, some of them long term, will be needed. They are variously described as structural, legal, attitudinal, organisational, financial or, more often, a complex mix of these and other factors for which the term 'cultural' is a convenient, if rather vague, blanket. Since educational policies and educational institutions form an integral part of modern society, drawing their goals, beliefs, practices and structures from society at large as much as from their own distinctive histories and modalities, it is necessary to take these broader social trends and values fully into account. Equity issues most intimately connect higher education with its wider social and cultural environment. Policies need to be both intensive and extensive.

If success in equity policies in higher education in countries of quite diverse political ideologies has been moderate or quite limited in some areas, and if rates of progress in achieving clearly defined – and sometimes well resourced – policy objectives is slow, it is necessary to reflect on underlying social dynamics which may not be susceptible to voluntaristic policy intervention. The realization of a societal goal requires introducing a change into societal relations and, as a rule, attempts to introduce change encounter some resistance. Unless this resistance is reduced, a course of action set will not be a course of action followed.

To minimise resistance, policies need to be well thought out, responsive to a variety of expressed preferences by groups and interested parties, clearly explained and justified, targeted, and resourced. Their implementation should be monitored and evaluated and adjusted if necessary to meet changing circumstances. Equity objectives directed at the advancement of particular groups—and procedures adopted in pursuit of these objectives—have been the most visible witnesses of the drive for greater equity in higher education. However, there have been two general developments which have had positive equity outcomes: (1) the massive increase in student enrolments and (2) the introduction or extension of institutional and programmatic differentiation in higher education (diversification). These developments, in addition to driving forward the equity movement, are in part an outcome of the broader community interest in a more equitable society.

Diversification in the province of higher education is the result of several factors of which efforts to equalize opportunity is but one – the separate, historical origins of more 'academic' and more 'vocational' institutions (often with a strong socio-economic class basis), demands of the industrial and service economy, finance (universities are usually more expensive), among them. However, inasmuch as differentiation not only of institutional type but also of programmes and ways of teaching and learning is a recognition of the different characteristics and needs of students and a determination to make higher education in some form more widely available, diversification can be an important factor in advancing equity policies. It ceases to be so when the channeling of students into different kinds of institutions is negatively discriminatory, when it reinforces existing inequalities. It then has the opposite, if unintended, effect of undermining the goals and values of equity.

STRATEGIES TO PROMOTE ACCESS AND EQUITY

The gains already made in achieving greater equity provide platforms for further progress. The different aspects and dimensions of equity, and the varied national and local settings in which policies are formulated and implemented indicate that a variety of approaches is required. While international experience and viewpoints among policy makers, researchers and commentators converge on a number of key considerations, caution is needed when transforming these into strategies of wider general applicability. The circumstances and needs of the several major under-represented groups obviously differ: what may be suitable for increasing participation in higher education by ethnic minority students may not the same as the requirements for improving study career opportunities for people with a disability. Moreover, in the higher education community within as well as between countries there are different expectations, structures and value orientations, and at times divergent views about appropriate policy mixes.

A significant limitation in drawing general conclusions for future action on the basis of 'international good practice' is the dearth of evaluative research on the impact of established policies and programme initiatives. Such research, to be valid and carry conviction, would need to be long term and comprehensive, taking account of the multiplicity of factors which, over time, bear on access, performance and professional advancement. There appears to be little interest in or ready support at present for such research, which means that for many of the interventions and particularly the recommendations for policy change, explanations and expectations regarding effect must be to a degree provisional.

Legislation, Monitoring and Compliance

In those countries with robust equity policies and programmes there has been strong state intervention: comprehensive, coherent policy making; equal opportunity and anti-discrimination legislation; and an effective regulatory and monitoring structure. The establishment of monitoring and compliance authorities, and of agencies to support innovations, and of commissions or quality agencies to review and evaluate the performance of higher education testify to the importance of strong central initiatives. Standing commissions and Ministry divisions to fund institutions and overview policy are coming to use financial inducements, incentives and sanctions. Firm, well-focused policies at the state and regional levels are proving their value.

The huge growth of the tertiary education sector world-wide has extended opportunities in varying degrees to all of the under-represented groups, including opportunities for careers in higher education. Equity goals are not the only driving force; moreover, gains have been uneven with some groups left behind. Large enrolment increases can be accompanied by poor retention and success rates. Continued overall volume growth of the sector remains, however, one of the most effective ways to achieve inclusiveness. It needs to incorporate targeted growth, e.g. of mature age entry, ethnic minorities.

Achieving Flexibility

A greater diversity of institutions and flexibility of provision are seen by the OECD and the European Community among other bodies as necessary as demand for and participation in tertiary education increase. This means broadening the concept of higher education to make it more inclusive and the adoption of more flexible forms of teaching and learning, recognition of prior learning, credit transfer, etc. Diversification policies can be used to improve access and study opportunities, for example for part-time and mature age students, those who do not meet normal entry criteria, for students with strong practical interests, those on low incomes and so on.

A great strength of tertiary education in the United States is its diversity. The community colleges for example are valued - by students who work, have children, are of modest means—for their affordability, flexible scheduling, convenience and personal attention. Many structural reforms across Europe since the 1960's have resulted in a wide variety of post-secondary institutions either within or providing access to higher education. In Belgium, Germany, the Netherlands and the UK where existing vocational institutions have been transformed into non-university higher education institutions and new institutions established.

Responsiveness to equity requirements is being shown right across the higher education sector in more course options, greater support and guidance for students with special needs, flexible scheduling, part-time and distance education, and so on – a growing readiness to adapt the educational system to the characteristics and circumstance of non-traditional students.

In some instances – for example with minority groups – there is beginning to be an acceptance that distinctive cultural features including valued symbols and rituals should feature rather than be suppressed under blanket, system-wide policies and conventional institutional procedures. The customs of particular groups can, for example, enliven graduation ceremonies – as when Australian Aboriginal graduate students are 'danced' by their communities to receive their diplomas at graduation ceremonies, a visible symbol of the community's 'ownership' of success.

Policy Coherence

Policy, structural and vertical programme coherence across the levels of education from early childhood to tertiary education is still often weak. It is extremely difficult to achieve across the major social sectors of education, health, welfare, housing, employment, etc. There is growing recognition that equity problems in higher education cannot be solved only at that stage or by an exclusive focus on educational opportunities. Early identification and intervention are necessary and at the school level, if progress is to be made in increasing the proportion of under-represented groups seeking and eligible for access at the tertiary level. The importance of policy coherence across sectors is shown, for example, in the kinds of support that need to be mobilised when people with a disability or women with family responsibilities with a low income and living in isolated areas seek access to tertiary education.

Mutual Advancement

Especially in the areas of women's education, opportunities for people with disabilities and mature age study in distance education institutions, experience has demonstrated the value of self help groups, and of networks which draw upon pooled experience, provide support and encouragement, and monitor the performance of the education system against their own goals and expectations.

Advances have been made as a result of well-organised lobby and pressure groups which, while they may be uncomfortable at times for institutions and governments, have been instrumental in identifying shortcomings and mobilising support in overcoming them. The women's movement has been most active and successful both in pressing for changes in course content, teaching and learning and in pursuing career advancement for women, including confidence building and leadership training events. Encouragement can be given to selfdefined under-represented groups to provide mutual support and organise their own projects for advancement.

Focus on Institutions

National policies, legislation, monitoring and compliance agencies, networks and self-help groups are crucial, but the equity heartland in higher education remains the institution. Measures which are having an effect include the annual reports on equity performance which all public universities make to the national ministry. Policies, procedures, values and ethos and the way of life of the institution are decisive in determining whether equity is achieved in practice.

Equity is the province of the whole institution. An illustration of this is admission policy. It is now common for institutions in many countries to accept professional experience in lieu of some formal qualifications, and to provide bridging courses - which may be by distance education, for example, for adults. Assessment practices can vary, to take into account special needs, such as the language of indigenous people, disability and off-campus study: cultural biases can be reduced in assessment practices, course materials and teaching procedures.

The spirit of the equity enterprise and the day-to-day reality of enhanced opportunity are experienced by students and staff as members of institutions. Hence the pay-off from those systems where the policy framework provides for - or requires - a clear demonstration by institutions of their actual performance in developing and implementing comprehensive equity programmes.

Institutions can achieve much by examining their own structures to identify specific needs and establish mechanisms to address them; such as appointing a special adviser to the rector or women's affairs; setting up a committee to review and report on progress in advancing its own equity mission; establishing a diagnostic and tutorial support centre for students; allocating a tranche of new post doctorate positions to women; establishing a centre for research and promotion which provides a national service.

Mainstream support, if broadly developed, can provide for many equity needs, avoiding wasteful duplication of specialist services. The role of institution leaders and governing bodies is crucial: in providing direction and support for equity policies, prominence in launching them and in follow through. The regular administrative reporting of progress to academic and faculty boards and governing bodies, against clearly stated equity objectives is an important contribution to institutional awareness and solidarity. Institutional leaders need to be publicly identified with equity policies. It is, as has often been remarked, the pattern of life that the student experiences at the institution that can make the difference between success and failure.

Performance Improvement

Where equity is identified as an important element in the overall quality, efficiency and performance of systems and institutions, it can be incorporated within a broader set of strategies, not seen as something special, separate from the institutional mainstream of teaching and research - and potentially contentious. This is partly a matter of definition; partly of goal-setting and resolution in execution; partly of monitoring, reporting and evaluative procedures. Benchmarking— in the more precise form of quantitative comparisons among institutions or across systems or more loosely as the use of a variety of instruments and procedures to appraise performance against some kind of comparative standard—is gaining ground in higher education in the quest for improved quality and efficiency.

Performance against equity criteria and goals can form part of benchmarking as of the many other evaluation procedures now commonly used in higher education systems. Drawbacks in highly targeted, specialist programmes, such as the problem of self-identification by some disabled and ethnic groups, or apparent unfairness in affirmative action, could be lessened with greater emphasis on a broad concept of quality and delivery to include equity. Incentives for improved performance measured against the institution's own goals are likely to achieve more than sanctions. More attention needs to be given to implementation and follow-up when conducting reviews whether institutional, national or international.

Financing, Resourcing and Managing

One of the challenges for effective implementation of equity policies is to meet the call for additional resources – for facilities and materials for students with a disability, for aid to needy students, for additional tutorial, technical and administrative resources, for mentoring, staff development, and for monitoring, evaluation and compliance. Some of these costs can be streamlined, for example, by inter-institutional co-operation in the design and provision of facilities, by consolidation into regional or national bases, and by more flexible use of specialist staff including sharing among institutions.

There is scope to interrelate and mainstream the different equity structures and programmes. Conversely, institutions can avoid costly litigation (whose incidence is growing) by adhering to antidiscrimination and equal opportunity legislation, and can attract additional funding (or avoid penalties) by meeting performance targets – as in the Danish taximeter and the Australian performance funding formulae. There are also substantial financial benefits to systems as well as institutions where courses are not unduly protracted, completion targets are met and dropout and failure rates are kept to a minimum. Financial incentives are becoming more common.

It is important for equity purposes to ensure that, in strict performance regimes, low performing students—and staff—are not excluded, but provided with opportunities to do well. The maintenance of high standards and the quest for excellence need not stand in the way of a rethinking of performance in acknowledgement of the greater diversity of the higher education population. While there are financial implications, it is poor economy to admit large numbers of students and then to accept high failure and dropout rates.

Towards Inclusive Policy Framework

Much of the work on advancing equity has been piecemeal, of necessity as some see it. The target groups are different, they have their own networks, financial sources, professional associations, and links with different parts of government. While retaining their distinctiveness, they could make further gains by exploring synergies.

Governments, policy-makers and institutions have an interest in achieving more effective, mutually reinforcing and streamlined programmes. There may be difficulties in balancing these moves with the very assertively defined distinctiveness of some under-represented groups, but there are gains to be made. The further development and refinement of frameworks for legislative changes, policy formulation, appeals and redress procedures, system-level monitoring, evaluation and follow through and other systemwide strategies can be expected to continue in respect of all under-represented groups. As well, a growing repertoire and pool of tested and evaluated 'hands-on' procedures will be used by practitioners in the field whether named equity officers, individual staff or institutional leaders and managers. There should develop, as a result, more comprehensive and systematic knowledge bases than exist at present, hence greater confidence in the effectiveness and results of specific interventions.

Many different agencies and actors are involved and there is no single authority, in any country, which is charged with responsibility for the kind of policy co-ordination and follow-through that would be required. However, a higher education co-ordinating and funding agency could play a major role in increasing awareness of the kinds of action that are needed—and may indeed be taking place—and, in conjunction with other responsible authorities, in vigorously pursuing all elements of a broad equity agenda.

For further equity gains to be made in higher education, different kinds of actions will be required at all levels of the education system and in the wider society. Partnerships and coalitions will be required together with legislative changes and more comprehensive policies.

Obviously higher education agencies and institutions can have only part of the responsibility for all this but they need to address their roles and responsibilities in a wider framework. Moreover, higher education needs to work more directly beyond its own immediate boundaries—with secondary schools, community groups, the professions (many of whose members it educates), employers and government. To illustrate the scale and the scope of action needed in the education system and leading up to and including higher education, there follows a table of needs, tasks and responsibilities. The challenge to higher education is to show initiative and leadership and to demonstrate commitment and success. Its role, for example in teacher education (but not only there) extends beyond its own immediate boundaries and in one way or another to all levels of the education system. Thus, the tertiary sector, in addition to attending to its own territory, needs to enlarge its role through a wide array of 'equity partnerships and extensions'.

Future Directions

At its simplest, most basic level, achieving greater equity in higher education is a matter of extending opportunity to participate and progress and using all possible, ethically sound means to do so. Widening opportunity for and in higher education has many benefits in strengthening democracy, achieving economic and social progress, advancing human rights, and improving the efficiency, quality and performance of the educational system. These matters are no longer in serious dispute. The task is to concentrate on ways and means, on improving data, evaluation and follow-through.

The expansion, broadening and diversification of higher education is one path to follow. The other is the hands-on encouraging, assisting and enabling of all who can benefit and contribute, whether as students, staff or both. A stronger, better evaluated knowledge base, greater clarity of purpose, and an increased readiness to consult and negotiate, are needed in policy making and implementation, alike.

A fair chance for all is a continuing goal which is realisable progressively, provided the different characteristics, needs, aspirations and circumstances of all the under-represented groups are well understood and well responded to. No less important, members of these groups have a responsibility to define their needs and interests and assist in their realisation in practice. Partnerships, collaborative measures, a sense of shared interests and common effort, and a readiness to reflect critically but constructively on progress achieved and gains yet to be made will continue to yield results. Although higher education alone cannot achieve all this, its roles can be strengthened to include a closer integration with the education system as a whole and partnerships with other social sectors.

The intellectual tradition to which higher education proudly adheres is the source of ideals, standards and procedures which are as pertinent to the quest for equity as the pursuit of academic excellence. The challenge is to bind them inextricably together as the enterprise of higher education inexorably expands and develops.All must contribute if policies are to be effective: individuals, institutions, governments, policy makers, special interest groups and those sections of government departments and specialist agencies that have a direct interest in or responsibility for equity in education in all its forms. The leadership role of institutional executives has been mentioned, but what of politicians, especially ministers and education and equity committee chairs, and what of the intermediary bodies responsible for funding, quality appraisal and steering?

Since the various equity movements are still well short of achieving their stated educational objectives - and this means, *inter alia,* that the objectives of national educational policies both general and sectoral are not being fully met - there must continue to be initiatives from several different quarters. Monitoring and ensuring compliance - and doing so with full effect - is a necessary and important role for agencies but compliance is not just a matter of bureaucratic efforts to enforce rules and regulations. A more inspirational, encouraging, challenging and supporting role needs to be performed. These are leadership responsibilities which fall within the competence and remit of the system-wide, policy making, regulating, compliance environment.

Better monitoring, more evaluative, analytical and transparent studies of the conditions affecting performance and the results of interventions, and greater visibility to the ways in which different areas of higher education policy are intermeshed will all help. They are valuable instruments and procedures to mobilise in order to provide public policy makers, agency officials and staff in institutions with the means to take a stronger leadership role and show initiative. They can thereby contribute to producing a more equitable higher education environment than exists now.

Construct and implement comprehensive, coherent policies addressing the full range of higher education equity issues; Set these higher education policies in the context of the lifelong learning chain, from early childhood to mature adulthood;

- Ensure that there is appropriate and adequate legislation and regulatory procedures with firm compliance measures;
- Have well developed procedures for setting targets, implementing, regularly monitoring and evaluating equity performance;
- Use financial instruments both system-wide and within institutions to recognise and encourage good practice;
- Work closely with the school system, community and professional bodies in well co-ordinated and targeted strategies to improve opportunities for under-represented groups;
- Ensure staff, physical resources and finance are adequate for the task, appropriately deployed to meet the targets that are set and comply with legal and regulatory requirements;

- Develop curricula and procedures for teaching and learning, assessment and student progress that meet equity goals including specific 'at risk' groups;
- Make full use of incentives, staff training and other forms of encouragement and recognition to bring about a strong institution-wide commitment to equity;
- Have observatories and procedures to identify and work systematically on major barriers, bottlenecks and problem areas;
- Mobilise staff and students to raise consciousness, improve knowledge and understanding, counter prejudice and gain publicity for equity achievements;
- Strengthen research, data and information capabilities, and resources, and use them in regular reports;
- Ensure that equity policies, programmes and issues regularly feature in strategic planning and the exercise of institutional governance, management and leadership;
- Be creative, thoughtful and energetic in developing and supporting inclusive cultures in higher education institutions.

Individual teachers and researchers will need to look beyond their disciplines to the moral purposes of education. Institutional administrators and leaders will need to provide encouragement and support for a wider vision than research outputs and specialised scientific and professional training. It is for public authorities and governments to provide the resources and ensure that the necessary policies and frameworks are in place. It is only through shared responsibility and concerted action that there can be further progress towards a more equitable system of higher education.

7

CHALLENGES OF HIGHER EDUCATION GOVERNANCE

There is little doubt that the university as we know it—the modern university as a project of the nation state and its cultural identity—finds itself in a complicated and indeed delicate situation at the moment. Universities are institutions that, in all societies, have performed basic functions which result from the particular combination of cultural and ideological, social and economic, educational and scientific roles that have been assigned to them. They are multi-purpose or multi-product institutions which contribute to the generation and transmission of ideology, the selection and formation of elites, the social development and educational upgrading of societies, the production and application of knowledge and the training of the highly skilled labour force.

This range of functions constitutes the key tasks of higher education systems, albeit with different emphases depending on the national context, the historical period, the specific sector and indeed the institution concerned. But what is clear is that nowadays, universities are heavily involved in literally every kind of social and economic activity in our increasingly dynamic societies—and this is one of the factors that make higher education such an interesting social institution to study.

Moreover, there is no prospect of achieving any kind of stability in university society relationships, let alone one which will satisfy all parties, for there seems no longer a single society to which a university can now be expected to respond. There are only governments, academics and students, labour markets and industries, professions and occupations, status groups and reference groups, communities and localities, and the dis-localities of the "global".

In this light it can be seen as of great analytic interest to study the emerging new modes of co-ordination in the higher education sector, their underlying rationales and in particular the effects of internationalisation and globalisation and also how these are being translated into institutional frameworks and responses. Equally, from a normative point of view it also seems essential to stimulate a policy search for institutions which will be solid and dynamic enough to withstand the current tensions and dilemmas: dilemmas that are already triggering demands for the simultaneous performance of contradictory functions in a polycentric and internationalising environment.

A review of the complex and dynamic processes of internationalisation at different levels in higher education reveals that these processes are prompting increasingly rapid change in two rather different respects. First, there is now a wide range of border-crossing activities, many of them resulting from institutional rather than governmental initiatives, and these are certainly still on the rise. But we can also see more substantial changes towards systematic national or supra-national policies, combined with a growing awareness of issues of international co-operation and competition in a globalising higher education market.

Under the first heading there is a growth of specific, clearly visible international co-operation, including activities such as student and staff mobility schemes, co-operative research activities and foreign language teaching to support them; under the second, we can see trends towards internationalisation, regionalisation or globalisation of the actualsubstance and structures of higher education—for example, proposals for convergence in institutional patterns, study programmes or curricula.

Perhaps at no time since the establishment of the universities in the medieval period has higher education been so international in scope. Internationalism is a key part of the future, and higher education is a central element in the knowledge-based global economy. Those who claim to have identified a strong trend towards internationalisation, are self-evidently also describing the past: asserting that higher education in the past was less international than today, and even less so in comparison with the anticipated future. A closer look, however, shows that higher education in the past can be described in a seemingly controversial and even contradictory way.

The university in its medieval Western tradition has always been perceived as a highly international institution compared to other major institutions of society. Grand notions of students moving freely from Bologna to Paris to Oxford suggest that from its earliest times the university transcended national or, to be more precise, territorial frontiers. These medieval folk-memories are reinforced by images of the Renaissance, of Europe in the Age of Enlightenment, and nowadays of academics as the archetypal global players in contemporary societies.

Certainly there has always been an appreciation of cosmopolitan values in universities, pride was frequently based on international recognition and reputation, international co-operation and mobility were not unusual, and a universal conception of knowledge dominated many disciplines and was seen as legitimate in others. Thus one could fairly argue that the university always was and still is an international institution, and that it has been a major force not only in the secularisation of modern societies but also in their internationalisation.

But these memories and images may actually serve as a kind of mystification if they are taken as proof that the university always has been, and therefore always will be, an international institution. The other side of the coin is the prominent historical role of universities in the process of nation-building, and their dependence on the nation state. In his essay on the modern university, Wittrock wrote that ... universities form part and parcel of the very same process which manifests itself in the emergence of an industrial economic order and the nation-state as the most typical and most important form of political organisation.

This is what the "nationalisation" of higher education is about. The contemporary university was born of the nation state, not of medieval civilisation, and it was only in the nineteenth and twentieth centuries, following the establishment of clear national economic interests, that universities acquired their identification with science and technology. Their regulatory and funding context was, and still is, national; their contribution to national cultures was, and still is, significant; students tended to be, and still are, trained to become national functionaries; and universities played, and still play, a considerable role in what some have called the military industrial complex of nation states.

In this perspective, they are very much national institutions. It is appropriate, therefore, to see current trends as part of a process by which national systems of higher education are being challenged by new forces of internationalisation. Universities are thus objects as well as subjects of "internationalisation" or "globalisation". They are affected by and at the same time influence these processes.

IMPACTS OF INTERNATIONALISATION

Having said this, the notion of internationalisation reminds us at the same time of its clear links to international power and domination. There are neo-colonial elements in the debate: nationalism may well be provoked into growth at times of internationalisation; competition and exclusion are at stake when terms such as "globalisation" are on the agenda. The narrative of globalisation that entered the English-speaking world in the 1960s, and was then taken up surprisingly quickly all over the world, is not just a narrative but an ideology with multiple meanings and linkages. In this context it is often constructed as an impersonal and inevitable force – sometimes in order to justify certain policies. At any event it should make us suspicious that the most powerful actors, and the most likely winners, praise internationalisation of higher education almost unconditionally, and push aside the anxieties of the less powerful actors.

The challenges of internationalisation or globalisation are confronting developing countries at a time of major national transformation and re-structuration. These countries' burden is in many cases threefold: to support the further expansion and "nationalisation" of their higher education system, to redefine its role and situation in the regional context, and to struggle with the impact of global forces confronting it, like the WTO treatment of higher education in the framework of the GATS agreements. Meanwhile, in many industrialised countries "internationalisation" and "globalisation" are nowadays performing a kind of "icebreaker" function for national reform agendas. In many cases, neither the diagnoses of the perceived problems of the system nor the corresponding prescriptions for reform are in any way new. But the international argument lends fresh wind to national debates on higher education reform which can now sail under the flag of "internationalisation" by claiming to strengthen national capacities in the face of global competition.

Thus an additional factor to be considered is competition among systems and institutions of higher education. At the institutional level, universities have not generally been perceived in the past as highly competitive: over the last half-century, the huge state-funded growth of higher education has damped down any need for competition. In any case, most institutions' capacity to compete was limited in practical terms, even if they might have wished to extend their territory.

The scenery is now being changed, first by the recent stagnation or even decrease in levels of financial support, which is sharpening institutions' need for new sources of funding, and second by the blurring of boundaries of space and time through the availability of new technologies which are making possible new modalities, both of learning and of research. So, as globalisation theorists would have it, the past is no longer a reliable guide to the future.

Despite earlier low levels of competition, the increasing rivalry among higher education institutions, along with the other competitive challenges just mentioned, is leading universities that wish to compete, or to find new niches in the emerging international market, to develop more adaptable and flexible means of organising and managing academic work.

These adaptations can take a variety of forms. In some universities we see newer and income-earning (and hence potentially competitive) activities such as continuing education, technology transfer and research exploitation taking place at, or even just beyond, the boundary: new units are created to manage these activities which leave the traditional core of academic work relatively untouched. In others, new structures are emerging which increase internal differentiation, and bring these activities more into the centre of the university while preserving or even sharpening the distinction between old and new roles.

Others again are aiming at various forms of integration, so that a new and more competitive culture begins to suffuse even the most traditional and stable areas of academic work. In other words, we might say that universities' reactions to internationalisation, and their hunger for new resources, begin as a series of blisters on their skins. It is an interesting question whether they can continue to treat these as localised eruptions to be plastered over orother-wise contained at the periphery, or whether they will be forced to adopt a more holistic approach.

At the national level, however, we can see two contradictory factors. On one hand, as suggested above, politicians are paying growing attention to international competition. On the other hand, there seems to be a growing concern with mutual observation and comparison between systems and institutions, which suggests a kind of revival of interest in international co-operation.

For policy analysts working in comparative higher education it is, of course, particularly interesting to see how a previously widespread and entrenched scepticism about the possibility of learning anything useful from foreign experiences is being overtaken by an equally insouciant optimism as to the transferability of specific elements of other higher education systems. The outcomes of this development, however intriguing, are far from clear. The advent of globalisation as a fashionable topic has led to considerable controversy over whether it is a genuine social process or a new element of political discourse—or, most plausibly, a composite mixture of both.

Globalisation sometimes seems a catch-all phrase or a non-concept, a catalogue of more or less everything that seems different since the 1970s: advances in information technology, greater capital flow across borders, international mobility of labour or of students, new public management and the weakening power of nation states, credit transfer in higher education and international recognition of degrees. Moreover, "globalisation", "internationalisation", "regionalisation" and "de-nationalisation" are frequently used interchangeably to highlight the international activities and widening outreach of higher education. Still, there are important differences and Scott has proposed a clearer distinction between the different terminologies.

The concept of internationalisation should refer mainly to processes of greater co-operation between states, and consequently to activities which take place across state borders. It reflects a world order in which nation states still play a central role. Given this political reality, the emphasis is on the building of strategic international relationships, based on mutual co-operation and also on mutual observation. In this formulation, the conceptual boundaries between the state, the market and the university seem fairly clear, albeit regularly contested in practice.

In contrast, globalisation refers primarily to the processes of increasing interdependence, and ultimately convergence, of economies, and to the liberalisation of trade and markets. (In addition and as an observable consequence, globalisation has a strong cultural component, which tends to encourage the establishment of a (usually Western) global-brand culture, although in principle it can also support the diffusion of more indigenous traditions.)

The process of globalisation is associated with a restructuring of the nation state: through the deregulation of legal and financial controls, the opening of markets or quasi-markets (including in higher education), and the increasing primacy of notions of competition, efficiency and managerialism. In a globalised environment, the power of nation states is fundamentally challenged: states find that they have very limited control over policies that regulate higher education "systems".

This basic distinction between internationalisation and globalisation can be supplemented, if also complicated, by the concept of "regionalisation". Taking Europe as an example, and regarding "Europeanisation" as a form of regionalisation, we can see two somewhat contradictory trends. On the one hand, regionalisation, at least in higher education, could be described as a process of growing regional cooperation or even integration on equal terms, involving mutual co-operation and "horizontal" interaction at all levels: between national and sub-national governments, between sectors and institutions of higher education across the region, and even region-wide collaboration among corresponding units within universities and colleges: in other words, a benign regional version of the internationalisation processes we have just described.

On the other hand, one can also make a persuasive case that regionalisation in higher education is part and parcel of the globalisation process, establishing co-operation among neighbours in order to counteract the pressure from other parts of the world.

Having said this, it seems obvious that globalisation and to some extent regionalisation as well tend to be regarded as dominant factors contributing to a certain "de-nationalisation" that affect important sectors in society, like higher education. The fall of the nation-state—whether it is political reality or not—can, however, have two distinct meanings. On the one hand, we can discuss issues related to shifts in the sovereignty of nation-states where responsibilities and capacities for political steering are moved to an international level and to a local level. On the other hand de-nationalisation might be discussed as a process of "de-etatisation" or "Entstaatlichung" due to certain rearrangements in the triangle between the state, the market, and forms of societal self-organisation. Discussions in this area thus focus on the transfer of authority and responsibility, either downwards (decentralisation, localisation), upwards (inter-, trans-nationalisation) or to the side (de-regulation, privatisation, self-organisation).

Some such attempt to reduce the bewildering variety of phenomena labelled "globalisation" to a more systematic definition must be an essential preliminary to any serious account of current developments. But if we are to move beyond definitions, there are a number of options. One option is to disentangle and systematise the various components and dimensions already addressed. Can we actually observe the phenomenon of "globalisation"? Where and how is it really happening? Is it producing convergence within higher education, and at what levels? Is it undermining the authority of nation states over higher education, and if so, where is all the power going? Is a global higher education system—and culture—genuinely in the making?

It ought to be obvious that our answers to these key questions in the globalisation debate may not necessarily all lead in the same directions. Recent developments seem, for example, to be leading to a society that is multidimensional, polycentric and contingent—but one, however, in which the national and the trans-national still coexist. As various studies have reminded us, the role of the state has changed, but it has not been eliminated. It is not simply the case that the national state is losing significance, because the state itself has been a key agent in the implementation of global processes, and it has emerged quite altered by this participation.

In this light, the controversy between "the state" and "the market" as imperfect alternatives may as well not be as sharp as it seems at first sight. While recent reforms have been prompted by a loss of trust in the regulatory power of the state and the widespread perception of so-called government failures, we now find a growing awareness of the imperfections of the market, including so-called market failures. It still remains to be seen what will happen in the longer run, now that in so many countries the state has decided to set up markets or quasi-markets in service sectors like higher education. And our understanding of globalisation is still in its infancy.

Both the challenges and the trends described above are beginning to influence the development of higher education policy at the national level. They are leading to initiatives that go beyond traditional internationalisation policies, which could be characterised as marginal, add-on activities mainly focused on the international mobility of students and teachers. We are now seeing more structural measures which will influence the higher education system more profoundly. Mutual awareness and self-reflexivity among the actors involved are certainly growing in the international landscape of higher education.

Moreover, globalisation does not have to be a uniform process and is not necessarily leading to uniform outcomes. We should bear in mind that the context for internationalisation varies substantially from country to country. As we all know, context matters, and the point we started from always leaves its stamp on wherever we may arrive.

The economic and political power of a country, its size and geographic location, its dominant culture, the quality and typical features of its higher education system, the role its language plays internationally, and previous internationalisation policies have all to be taken into consideration. Not so many years ago, many countries had sharply differing views on the merits or even the possibility of internationalisation, and the same can still be said today—even if to a somewhat lesser extent.

Studies like these should make us aware of the usefulness of comparative research in higher education. Comparative perspectives on governmental policies of the nation-state and on national systems of higher education still offer fruitful cross-national insights into national patterns. They are as well ... indispensable for understanding a reality shaped by common international trends, reforms based on comparative observation, growing trans-national activities and partial supra-national integration in higher education.

But the underlying rationale of traditional forms of comparative higher education research is a presumption that we can reasonably analyse and compare national systems which are defined as relatively closed; and this is being challenged by recent trends. Given the complexity of the phenomena involved, we may need to keep an open mind as researchers, and try to construct a more differentiated picture of the causes, implications, and effects of the emerging secular trends at stake and the multiplying actors and stakeholders involved. One such attempt may be found in governance studies.

GOVERNANCE OF ACADEMIC COMMONS

Mayntz has recently summarised the overall evolution or development of a theory of political governance, a theory that began by being concerned with the steering actions of political authorities as they deliberately attempt to shape socioeconomic structures and processes. She does so without special reference to given fields or sectors of policy studies, like higher education. A first attempt to follow respective developments in our field reveals, however, that higher education studies have not only reflected but contributed to this debate and helped to build a framework for the study of political governance.

In this context it is, of course, impossible to refer to or to document these developments by extensive references. An account to look for the contribution of higher education policy studies to the overall development of governance theory can rather serve to put our field into a larger context and to see to what extent this context might serve our further purposes of studying the international dimension in higher education.

For Mayntz "the modern theory of political governance emerged after World War II at a time when governments aspired explicitly to steer their nations' social and economic development in the direction of defined goals."The first paradigm of a theory of political governance was concerned with policy development and policy implementation, and it adopted a top-down, or legislator's perspective. A brief sketch of the evolution of this theory of political governance in the narrow sense of "steering" in higher education studies mirrors indeed very much the developments in other fields of policy analyses in three stages from "planning" via "policy development" to "policy implementation". Early studies in the late 1960s began with a largely prescriptive theory of planning of higher education. They were accompanied by strong believes in human capital and manpower planning approaches as well as the contribution of educational investment to economic growth.

In the 1970s, with the planning euphoria waning and the reform of higher education systems in Europe on the move, policy development became the object of empirical analyses; this directed attention to context factors influencing policy development, in particular executive organisation; different policy instruments were discussed, in particular the role of law. Finally, in the first half of the 1980s, policy implementation became a new research focus in higher education studies where the process of policy formulation, reformulation and implementation gained interest. These studies carried in themselves the seeds of their own transformation. Implementation research called attention to the fact of policy failure or shortcomings, and proved that such failure was not only the consequence of mistakes in planning or of shortcomings on the part of implementation agencies, but of having neglected specific characteristics of the field of policy implementation concerned as well as the recalcitrance of the target groups of public policy and their ability to resist or subvert the achievement of policy goals.

This recognition led to two important enlargement of the initial paradigm. First, had it so far concentrated on the subject of political steering, government and its ability or inability to steer, it now included also the structure and behavioural dispositions of the object of political control—the higher education system and its organisational structures. Important studies were undertaken to deepen our understanding of the systemic peculiarities of higher education, their embeddedness in professional believe systems and national traditions and ideosyncracies. Furthermore, the rise of studies in the sociology of organisations emphasised characteristics of universities' internal life and the nature of the relationship between their internal and external life that make these organisations unique and a significant object of study. Examples are 'loose coupling', 'organisational saga' and 'garbage can decision-making'. Thus the top-down perspective of the initial paradigm (policy making and implementation) was extended by the inclusion of questions related to the 'governability' of higher education systems as well as bottom-up processes which are in turn conditioned by the structure of the given regulatory field of higher education. This expansion of the analytical perspective taught us much about the conditions of policy effectiveness.

Second, the disappointment of the belief in the existence of an effective political control centre as well as the withdrawal of several states across Europe from direct control to 'steering from a distance' directed attention to alternative forms of governance: In various lines of discussion, market principles and horizontal self-organisation were discussed as alternatives to hierarchical political control.

Among the first and most often cited attempts is, of course, Clark's triangle of higher education systems between the three axes of market-like co-ordination, state-induced co-ordination, and academic/professional co-ordination. For some time it seemed—at least in the European context—as if "the state and the market" could be treated as alternative options in a kind of zero sum game—the more there is of one, the less there is of the other.

Analyses and differentiation between 'state control models' and 'state supervising models' as well as a perceived shift from 'ex ante control' of higher education to 'ex post control' contributed to a large extent to the understanding of the 'rise of the evaluative state' in higher education. They made it clear that we are dealing with not so much a loss of state control, but rather a change in its form. Recent critic of previous governance models, however, extended again the principle list of modes of coordination.Moreover, local self-governance, hierarchical self-steering, quasi-market competition, authoritative interaction and stakeholderism in higher education are no longer seen as exclusive or as alternative options—they coexist and are casually interrelated. At the same time, one might say that realism has grown as regards the potentials and limits of the steering capacities of certain modes of coordination.

Governmental failures as well as professional failures, market failures as well as managerial failures tend to be observed and it is not unlikely that network failures will enter the floor soon as well. Recently, the term "governance" has thus been extended in two ways, both distinct from political guidance or steering. For one thing, "governance" is now often used to indicate a new mode of governing that is distinct from the hierarchical control model, a more cooperative mode where state and non-state actors participate in mixed networks. Attempts at collective problem-solving outside of existing hierarchical frameworks of the nation-state have contributed significantly to this shift in the meaning of the term governance.

The second "new" meaning of the term governance is much more general, and has a different genealogy. Here governance means the different modes of coordinating individual actions, or basic forms of social order. Having arrived at this point, the basic frame of a theory of political governance seems complete—even though a lot remains to be done to study the complex relationships and dynamics of the different modes of co-ordination in (national) governance studies on higher education and cross-national comparisons. But meanwhile new problems have arisen, notably the crisis of the welfare state that is connected with European integration and economic globalisation. In the light of Europeanisation and globalisation, certain accepted and apparently unproblematic features of the previously sketched theory of governance and its application in the field of higher education studies appear suddenly as deficits, ". . . deficits which can trigger a new phase in theory development by challenging us to extend our analytical frame once more".

The deficits in question are:

– the concentration on the single nation state (even where international comparisons are made), and a selective concern with domestic politics.
– the concentration on policy effects on the changing relationship between the state and higher education organisations, and the internal governance of higher education institutions, neglecting the input side of policy formation, and the relationship between both.
– the concern with macro level policy-making and meso level organisational adaptation, neglecting to some extend the micro dynamics and effects in the actual practices and performances of academic work.

The theory of political governance has so far dealt with political systems that have a clear identity, a clear boundary, and a defined membership which implies specific rights and duties. This kind of approach is incapable of dealing with the problems raised by European integration, and especially with the problems raised by globalisation.

> "The formation of the European Union has established a new, transnational governance structure. The European Union is decidedly more than a regime, a contractual frame or a negotiating arena, but it is as clearly not a

> federal state; it can best be described as a complex multi-level system whose dynamics cannot well be understood in the conceptual frame developed for the analysis of political governance in nation states . . . For a theory of political governance, European integration has two consequences: (1) it raises new problems of governance on the national level, and (2) it requires the extension of governance theory to a supranational level."

The shift of powers to the European level requires us to study the effect of European directives upon the national higher education system and respective policies. This is in fact partly being done by several first studies in this area. In this way the previous paradigm is extended once again, this time by adding an important external factor of policy formation and implementation.

Recent research in this area shows that although variation across European Union countries prevails, national policies for internationalisation of higher education increasingly emphasise the economic benefits involved. A growing range of countries are aware of the increasing international competition in higher education and have formulated economic rationales for their internationalisation policies.

Furthermore, and very much related to the follow-up of the Bologna Declaration, the international and especially the European dimension is now becoming much more integrated into the main-stream national-level policy making on higher education. Furthermore, a European-wide survey of the follow-up process of the Bologna Declaration has demonstrated that the system-level reforms resulting from this process are leading to more convergence in terms of degree structures. At the same time, however, and due to the fact that the responsibility for the implementation rests with the individual countries, certain diversities certainly remain.

We can also observe the growth of a field called "European policymaking" in governance studies of mutual interdependence between national and European policy processes in a multi-level system. Here again, some studies on higher education have been undertaken that tend to underline the variety of policy-approaches to be observed in the peculiar case of higher education, i.e. the principle of subsidiarity and the segmented responsibility for education and training on the one hand, and science and research on the other hand. They are up-to-now, however, only loosely related to respective theoretical developments in other policy fields.

The default mode of Europeanised policy responses in higher education might for example been called "mutual adjustment". Here, national governments continue to adopt their own national policies, but they do so in response to, or anticipation of, the policy choices of other governments or certain perceived European developments.

At another level, European governance in higher education might be realised by "intergovernmental negotiations" where national policies are coordinated by agreements at the European level, but national governments try to remain in full control of the decision process, transformation into national contexts and implementation remains under their control.

The cooperation of countries in the Bologna process can be considered as such a governance form: a voluntary process, not binding and thus with no legal consequences for countries, institutions or students as compared to the EU processes of supranational steering or "hierarchical direction", although with very limited competences and authority in higher education. Another approach might be labelled "joint decisions" and combines intergovernmental negotiations and supranational direction. Here,

European legislation or initiative depends on action taken by the European commission but involves as well inter-governmental negotiations, increasingly the European Parliament as well as a heavy load of European comitology. The recent announcement towards the "European Research Area" and the call for the establishment of so-called "networks of excellence" in selected spearhead fields of research in the 6th Framework Program of the European Commission can serve as an example for this mode.

It would be certainly of interest to study the input side of policy formation as well as the outcome and output of this process, and the relationship between the two. Moreover, this recent development may be seen as complementing the European Union's policy objective for a "European Educational Area", put forward in the beginning of 1990s. It follows, however, a different logic of the overall policy process, and it is very unclear at the moment whether and how these two processes—crelated on the one hand to the educational function and on the other hand to the research function of higher education are going to be linked or integrated.

The above policies, developed in one or the other way at the European level, and forming part of the broader process of European integration, have, however, resulted in the emergence of a multi-level and multi-actor context within which higher education organisations operate and develop themselves their international activities. Previous evaluations and empirical research suggest that the organisational responses to national and European policies for internationalisation are far from uniform. Variation in organisational responses may refer to volume of international activities carried out, expansion across an organisation or across different organisations, the type of internationalisation of those activites, and the specific form that internationalisation takes, within the diversity of higher education organisations, systems, and national contexts.

Further studies on the perceptions of the European policies and the responses to these policies on the part of the actors of national policies and the key actors in the individual institutions of higher education are needed. Moreover, colleges and universities are increasingly international and at the same time local actors. International marketing of degrees and programmes, international network building and consortia, recruitment of international students and staff are among those factors contributing to a growing role of organisations as international agents. They underline a need for the study of how local actors and organisations extend their activities to the international stage.

Finally, concern with European policy-making also calls attention to another blind spot of national and cross-national governance studies in higher education: the microlevel of academic work and life. It is true that interest in studies on the academic profession has recently grown and that a number of studies have tried to analyse the impact of changing modes of coordination in higher education on the academic workplace in cross-national perspectives. Some of them tend to send out alarming signals: standards are compromised and curiosity is displaced, control is dispersed and coherence is lost, continuity diminishes and constant change produces stress. Others tend to support continuity rather than dramatic change as regards the self-image of academics, aspects of faculty morale or the major work tasks of the academic profession.

Most of them share, however, a macro-level perspective on policy making, management and international trends in higher education that concentrates on the upper levels of policy analyses. More fine grained analyses of the extent to which change at the academic workplace level is taking place is provided by Henkel in her national case study on academic identities and policy change in the UK.

The major challenge in this area will thus be to go further 'from theory to practice', i.e. to analyse the impact of changing governance structures and institutional environment on the identities, rules, and rewards that govern the academic commons as the principal internal constituencies of the higher education fabric. This is obviously a difficult and challenging task for further research.

All debates on the impact of recent developments and trends on the university can, however, not confine themselves in aiming to explore what suits best the public expectations, the managerial beliefs in functioning of modern organisations, or the job satisfaction of the academic profession. Even though the impact of external and internal changes on the daily practices and the performance of academe cannot easily be examined, and even though the battle on the definition and measurement of 'quality' of academic work is part of the ongoing change in higher education, we should not loose sight of the fact that they are the ultimate criteria. Further cross-national research along this line that includes several aspects of international academic labour and employment markets is certainly needed.

GOVERNANCE IN A GLOBALISING CONTEXT

While governance theory as well as higher education policy analysis have responded, at least partly, to the challenges which Europeanisation poses, this does not equally hold true for the process called globalisation. For all the talk about globalisation in higher education, there is limited theoretical conceptualisation as well as limited empirical study if and how it happens. Studies in that area tend for example to draw on theories derived from world system theory, international relation studies and organisational ecology/population theory. They show how certain policy discourses in higher education emerge and diffuse around the globe, and how they are locally 'adapted'.

Marginson and Rhoades have recently argued toward a "glonacal agency heuristic" to conceptualise the study of simultaneous significance of global, national, and local forces in higher education. Respective approaches come close to what others would call a multi-level perspective in actor-centered neo-institutionalism: a complex framework that conceptualises policy processes from a multi-level and multi-actor perspective driven by the interaction of individual and corporate actors endowed with certain capabilities and specific cognitive and normative orientations, within a given institutional setting and within a given external situation. Such studies lead us further to the frontiers of the state of the art of what we have tried to elaborate in this chapter as governance theory. They lead us as well to the major challenges we have to face in a multi-level and multi-actor study of global forces in higher education.

There is, first of all, the sheer complexity of transnational policy making and its interdependency with the national and local level. If globalisation is in the making, it probably means a growing disjunction between increasingly unbounded and farflung economic, social, and communicative networks on the one hand, and bounded political systems on the other hand, a disjunction between problem structures and (traditional) political structures. This is probably one of the reasons for the efforts to create and strengthen transnational regulatory frameworks, like regional blocs and associations such as the European Union or the North

American Free Trade Agreement or non-governmental organisations, such as ILO, OECD, UNESCO, WHO, or the World Bank. They mirror, at least, to some extent governance subjects and structures where it is, in principle, still possible to speak of a policy process with its input and output aspects. But there are furthermore many international organisations, like professional associations, interest organisations and scientific organisations.

There seem to be a rise of transnational epistemic communities and social movements, social groups without clear geographical reference. Given their co-existence with national and local agents and organisations, this creates an enormous complexity of the co-existence of many different types of structures and processes, i.e. different governance modes. It is thus not surprising to note that in the global market, most agents believe to play, as it were, most of the time "against nature". There is a danger that we ascribe our explanatory models for a structurally diffuse context to easily to specific forces thus contributing to a certain flavour of "conspiracy theory" that is as well easily around when it comes to globalisation.

This leads us to a second challenge. If globalisatition is in the making, it does not necessarily mean a linear and uniform process with uniform outcomes. Up-to-now higher education studies tend to emphasise globalisation if and when observations of "commonalities", "similar processes", "common structures", "one nation after the other" tend to be observed. A central tenet is that global reality is singular, and conforms everywhere to the same external laws. A corollary is that context is thought of as a set of conditional variables that have predicable effects under a general theory of a globalising world. Once the general developments are well understood, a full understanding of behaviour and institutions devolves.

But even if we assume certain global forces on and in higher education, like massification, neo-liberal politics, or ICT, they are not uniform but multidimensional. They develop in a world of unsimultaneity that will not be affected to the same extent and at the same point in time. Yet, it should be possible, even as we might note the global spread of standardised educational models, to perceive persistent pecularities of higher education systems and distinct national options.

8

UNESCO/OECD GUIDELINES FOR QUALITY PROVISION IN CROSS-BORDER HIGHER EDUCATION

INTRODUCTION

Purpose of the Guidelines

The Guidelines aim to support and encourage international cooperation and enhance the understanding of the importance of quality provision in cross-border higher education. The purposes of the Guidelines are to protect students and other stakeholders from low-quality provision and disreputable providers as well as to encourage the development of quality cross-border higher education that meets human, social, economic and cultural needs.

Rationale for the Guidelines

Since the 1980s, cross-border higher education through the mobility of students, academic staff, programmes/institutions and professionals has grown considerably. In parallel, new delivery modes and cross-border providers have appeared, such as campuses abroad, electronic delivery of higher education and for-profit providers.

These new forms of cross-border higher education offer increased opportunities for improving the skills and competencies of individual students and the quality of national higher education systems, provided they aim at benefiting the human, social, economic and cultural development of the receiving country.

While in some countries the national frameworks for quality assurance, accreditation and the recognition of qualifications take into account cross-border higher education, in many countries they are still not geared to addressing the challenges of cross-border provision. Furthermore, the lack of comprehensive frameworks for coordinating various initiatives at the international level, together with the diversity and unevenness of the quality assurance and accreditation systems at the national level, create gaps in the quality assurance of cross-border higher education, leaving some cross-border higher education provision outside any framework of quality assurance and accreditation. This makes students and other stakeholders more vulnerable to low-quality provision and disreputable providers of cross-border higher education. The challenge faced by current quality assurance and accreditation systems is to develop appropriate procedures and systems to cover foreign providers and programmes (in addition to national providers and programmes) in order to maximize the benefits and limit the potential drawbacks of the internationalization of higher education. At the same time, the increase in cross-border student, academic staff, researcher and professional mobility has put the issue of the recognition of academic and professional qualifications high on the international cooperation agenda.

There is therefore a need for additional national initiatives, strengthened international cooperation and networking, and more transparent information on procedures and systems of quality assurance, accreditation and the recognition of qualifications. These efforts should have a global range and should emphasize supporting the needs of developing countries to establish robust higher education systems. Given that some countries lack comprehensive frameworks for quality assurance, accreditation and the recognition of qualifications, capacity-building should form an important part of the overall strengthening and coordination of national and international initiatives. In this light, the UNESCO Secretariat and OECD have worked closely together in the development of these Guidelines for quality provision in cross-border higher education. The implementation of these Guidelines could serve as a first step in the capacity-building process.

The quality of a country's higher education sector and its assessment and monitoring is not only key to its social and economic well-being, it is also a determining factor affecting the status of that higher education system at the international level. The establishment of quality assurance systems has become a necessity, not only for monitoring quality in higher education delivered within the country, but also for engaging in delivery of higher education internationally. As a consequence, there has been an impressive rise in the number of quality assurance and accreditation bodies for higher education in the past two decades. However, existing national quality assurance capacity often focuses exclusively on domestic delivery by domestic institutions. The increased cross-border mobility of students, academic staff, professionals, programmes and providers presents challenges for existing national quality assurance and accreditation frameworks and bodies as well as for the systems for recognizing foreign qualifications. Some of these challenges are described below:

(a) National capacity for quality assurance and accreditation often does not cover cross-border higher education. This increases the risk of students falling victim to misleading guidance and information and disreputable providers, dubious quality assurance and accreditation bodies and low-quality provision, leading to qualifications of limited validity;

(b) National systems and bodies for the recognition of qualifications may have limited knowledge and experience in dealing with cross-border higher education. In some cases, the challenge becomes more complicated as cross-border higher education providers may deliver qualifications that are not of comparable quality to those which they offer in their home country;

(c) The increasing need to obtain national recognition of foreign qualifications has posed challenges to national recognition bodies. This in turn, at times, leads to administrative and legal problems for the individuals concerned;

(d) The professions depend on trustworthy, high-quality qualifications. It is essential that users of professional services including employers have full confidence in the skills of qualified professionals. The increasing possibility of obtaining low-quality qualifications could harm the professions themselves, and might in the long run undermine confidence in professional qualifications.

Scope of the Guidelines

The Guidelines aim to provide an international framework for quality provision in cross-border higher education that responds to the above-mentioned challenges.

The Guidelines are based on the principle of mutual trust and respect among countries and on the recognition of the importance of international collaboration in higher education. They also recognize the importance of national authority and the diversity of higher education systems. Countries attach a high importance to national sovereignty over higher education. Higher education is a vital means for expressing a country's linguistic and cultural diversity and also for nurturing its economic development and social cohesion. It is therefore recognized that policy-making in higher education reflects national priorities. At the same time, it is recognized that in some countries, there are several competent authorities in higher education.

The effectiveness of the Guidelines largely depends on the possibility of strengthening the capacity of national systems to assure the quality of higher education. The development and implementation of the UNESCO regional conventions and further support to the ongoing capacity-building initiatives of UNESCO, other multilateral organizations and bilateral donors in this area will sustain and be complementary to the Guidelines. These initiatives should be supported by strong regional and national partners.

The Guidelines acknowledge the important role of non-governmental organizations such as higher education associations, student bodies, academic staff associations, networks of quality assurance and accreditation bodies, recognition and credential evaluation bodies and professional bodies in strengthening international cooperation for quality provision in cross-border higher education. The Guidelines aim to encourage the strengthening and coordination of existing initiatives by enhancing dialogue and collaboration among various bodies. Cross-border higher education encompasses a wide range of modalities from face-to-face (taking various forms such as students travelling abroad and campuses abroad) to distance learning (using a range of technologies and including e-learning). In implementing the Guidelines, consideration should be given to the variety of provision and its different demands for quality assurance.

GUIDELINES FOR HIGHER EDUCATION STAKEHOLDERS

With due regard to the specific division of responsibilities in each country, the Guidelines recommend actions to six stakeholders: governments; higher education institutions/ providers including academic staff; student bodies; quality assurance and accreditation bodies; academic recognition bodies; and professional bodies.

Guidelines for Governments

Governments can be indfluential, if not responsible, in promoting adequate quality assurance, accreditation and the recognition of qualifications. They undertake the role of policy coordination in most higher education systems. However, it is acknowledged throughout these Guidelines that in some countries, the authority for overseeing quality assurance lies with subnational government bodies or with non-governmental organizations.

In this context, it is recommended that governments:

(a) Establish, or encourage the establishment of a comprehensive, fair and transparent system of registration or licensing for cross-border higher education providers wishing to operate in their territory;

(b) Establish, or encourage the establishment of a comprehensive capacity for reliable quality assurance and accreditation of cross-border higher education provision, recognizing that quality assurance and accreditation of cross-border higher education provision involves both sending and receiving countries;

(c) Consult and coordinate among the various competent bodies for quality assurance and accreditation both nationally and internationally;

(d) Provide accurate, reliable and easily accessible information on the criteria and standards for registration, licensure, quality assurance and accreditation of cross-border higher education, their consequences on the funding of students, institutions or programmes, where applicable, and their voluntary or mandatory nature;

(e) Consider becoming party to and contribute to the development and/or updating of the appropriate UNESCO regional conventions on the recognition of qualifications and establish national information centres as stipulated by the conventions;

(f) Where appropriate develop or encourage bilateral or multilateral recognition agreements, facilitating the recognition or equivalence of each country's qualifications based on the procedures and criteria included in mutual agreements;

(g) Contribute to efforts to improve the accessibility at the international level of up-to-date, accurate and comprehensive information on recognized higher education institutions/providers.

Guidelines for Higher Education Institutions/Providers

Commitment to quality by all higher education institutions/ providers is essential. To this end, the active and constructive contributions of academic staff are indispensable. Higher education institutions are responsible for the quality as well as the social, cultural and linguistic relevance of education and the standards of qualifications provided in their name, no matter where or how it is delivered.

In this context, it is recommended that higher education institutions/providers delivering cross-border higher education:

(a) Ensure that the programmes they deliver across borders and in their home country are of comparable quality and that they also take into account the cultural and linguistic sensitivities of the receiving country. It is desirable that a commitment to this effect should be made public;

(b) Recognize that quality teaching and research is made possible by the quality of faculty and the quality of their working conditions that foster independent and critical enquiry. The UNESCO Recommendation concerning the Status of Higher Education Teaching Personnel and other relevant instruments need to be taken into account by all institutions and providers to support good working conditions and terms of service, collegial governance and academic freedom;

(c) Develop, maintain or review current internal quality management systems so that they make full use of Guidelines for Quality Provision in Cross-border Higher Education the competencies of stakeholders such as academic staff, administrators, students and graduates and take full responsibility for delivering higher education qualifications comparable in standard in their home country and across borders. Furthermore, when promoting their programmes to potential students through agents, they should take full responsibility to ensure that the information and guidance provided by their agents are accurate, reliable and easily accessible;

(d) Consult competent quality assurance and accreditation bodies and respect the quality assurance and accreditation systems of the receiving country when delivering higher education across borders, including distance education;

(e) Share good practices by participating in sector organizations and inter-institutional networks at national and international levels;

(f) Develop and maintain networks and partnerships to facilitate the process of recognition by acknowledging each other's qualifications as equivalent or comparable;

(g) Where relevant, use codes of good practice such as the UNESCO/Council of Europe 'Code of good practice in the provision of transnational education' and other relevant codes such as the Council of Europe/UNESCO 'Recommendation on Criteria and Procedures for the Assessment of Foreign Qualifications';

(h) Provide accurate, reliable and easily accessible information on the criteria and procedures of external and internal quality assurance and the academic and professional recognition of qualifications they deliver and provide complete descriptions of programmes and qualifications, preferably with descriptions of the knowledge, understanding and skills that a successful student should acquire. Higher education institutions/providers should collaborate especially with quality assurance and accreditation bodies and with student bodies to facilitate the dissemination of this information;

(i) Ensure the transparency of the financial status of the institution and/or educational programme offered.

Guidelines for Student Bodies

As representatives of the direct recipients of cross-border higher education and as part of the higher education community, student bodies bear the responsibility of helping students and potential students to carefully scrutinize the information available and giving sufficient consideration in their decision-making process. In this context, it is recommended that the emergence of autonomous, local, national and international student bodies should be encouraged and that the student bodies:

(a) Be involved as active partners at international, national and institutional levels in the development, monitoring and maintenance of the quality provision of cross-border higher education and take the necessary steps to achieve this objective;

(b) Take active part in promoting quality provision, by increasing the awareness of the students of the potential risks such as misleading guidance and information, low quality provision leading to qualifications of limited validity, and disreputable providers. They should also guide them to accurate and reliable information sources on cross-border higher education. This could be done by increasing the awareness of the existence of these guidelines as well as taking an active part in their implementation;

(c) Encourage students and potential students to ask appropriate questions when enrolling in cross-border higher education programmes. A list of relevant questions could be established by student bodies, including foreign students where possible, in collaboration with bodies such as higher education institutions, quality assurance and accreditation bodies and academic recognition bodies. Such a list should include the following questions: whether the foreign institution/provider is recognized or accredited by a trustworthy body and whether the qualifications delivered by the foreign institution/ provider are recognized in the students' home country for academic and/or professional purposes.

Guidelines for Quality Assurance and Accreditation Bodies

In addition to internal quality management of institutions/providers, external quality assurance and accreditation systems have been adopted in more than 60 countries. Quality assurance and accreditation bodies are responsible for assessing the quality of higher education provision. The existing systems of quality assurance and accreditation often vary from country to country and sometimes within the countries themselves. Some have governmental bodies for quality assurance and accreditation, and others have non-governmental bodies. Furthermore, some differences exist in the terminologies used, the definition of 'quality', the purpose and function of the system including its link to the funding of students, institutions or programmes, the methodologies used in quality assurance and accreditation, the scope and function of the responsible body or unit, and the voluntary or compulsory nature of participation. While respecting this diversity, a coordinated effort among the bodies of both sending and receiving countries is needed at both the regional and global levels, in order to tackle the challenges raised by the growth of cross-border provision of higher education, especially in its new forms. In this context, it is recommended that quality assurance and accreditation bodies:

(a) Ensure that their quality assurance and accreditation arrangements include cross-border education provision in its various modes. This can mean giving attention to assessment guidelines, ensuring that standards and processes are transparent, consistent and appropriate to take account of the shape and scope of the national higher education system, and adaptability to changes and developments in cross-border provision;

(b) Sustain and strengthen the existing regional and international networks or establish regional networks in regions that do not already have one. These networks can serve as platforms to exchange information and good practice, disseminate knowledge, increase the understanding of international developments and challenges as well as to improve the professional expertise of their staff and quality assessors. These networks could also be used to improve awareness of disreputable providers and dubious quality assurance and accreditation bodies, and to develop monitoring and reporting systems that can lead to their identification;

(c) Establish links to strengthen the collaboration between the bodies of the sending country and the receiving country and enhance the mutual understanding of different systems of quality assurance and accreditation. This may facilitate the process of assuring the quality of programmes delivered across borders and institutions operating across borders while respecting the quality assurance and accreditation systems of the receiving countries;

(d) Provide accurate and easily accessible information on the assessment standards, procedures, and effects of the quality assurance mechanisms on the funding of students, institutions or programmes where applicable as well as the results of the assessment. Quality assurance and accreditation bodies should collaborate with other actors, especially higher education institutions/ providers, academic staff, student bodies and academic recognition bodies to facilitate the dissemination of such information;

(e) Apply the principles reflected in current international documents on cross-border higher education such as the UNESCO/Council of Europe 'Code of Good Practice in the Provision of Transnational Education';

(f) Reach mutual recognition agreements with other bodies on the basis of trust in and understanding of each other's professional practice, develop systems of internal quality assurance and regularly undergo external evaluations, making full use of competencies of stakeholders. Where feasible, consider undertaking experiments in international evaluation or peer reviews of quality assurance and accreditation bodies;

(g) Consider adoption of procedures for the international composition of peer review panels, international benchmarking of standards, criteria and assessment procedures and undertake joint assessment projects to increase the comparability of evaluation activities of different quality assurance and accreditation bodies.

Guidelines for Academic Recognition Bodies

The UNESCO regional conventions on recognition of qualifications are important instruments facilitating the fair recognition of higher education qualifications, including the assessment of foreign qualifications resulting from cross-border mobility of students, skilled professionals and cross-border provision of higher education.

There is a need to build on existing initiatives with additional international action to facilitate fair processes of recognition of academic qualifications by making systems more transparent and comparable.

In this context, it is recommended that academic recognition bodies:

(a) Establish and maintain regional and international networks that can serve as platforms to exchange information and good practice, disseminate knowledge, increase the understanding of international developments and challenges and improve the professional expertise of their staff;

(b) Strengthen their cooperation with quality assurance and accreditation bodies to facilitate the process of determining whether a qualification meets basic quality standards, as well as to engage in cross-border cooperation and networking with quality assurance and accreditation bodies. This cooperation should be pursued both at regional and cross-regional levels;

(c) Establish and maintain contacts with all stakeholders to share the information and improve the links between academic and professional qualification assessment methodologies;

(d) Where appropriate, address the professional recognition of qualifications in the labour market and provide necessary information on professional recognition, both to those who have a foreign qualification and to employers. Guidelines for Quality Provision in Cross-border Higher Education Given the increasing scope of the international labour markets and growing professional mobility, collaboration and coordination with professional associations are recommended for this purpose;

(e) Use codes of practice such as the Council of Europe/ UNESCO 'Recommendation on Criteria and Procedures for the Assessment of Foreign Qualifications' and other relevant codes of practice to increase the public's confidence in their recognition procedures, and to reassure stakeholders that the processing of requests is conducted in a fair and consistent manner;

(f) Provide clear, accurate and accessible information on the criteria for the assessment of qualifications, including qualifications resulting from cross-border provision.

Guidelines for Professional Bodies

Systems of professional recognition differ from country to country and from profession to profession. For example, in some cases, a recognized academic qualification could be sufficient for entry into professional practice, whereas in other cases, additional requirements are imposed on holders of academic qualifications in order to enter the profession. Given the increasing scope of international labour markets and growing professional mobility, the holders of academic qualifications, as well as employers and professional associations are facing many challenges. Increasing transparency – i.e., improving the availability and the quality of the information – is critical for fair recognition processes. In this context, it is recommended that professional bodies responsible for professional recognition:

(a) Develop information channels that are accessible both to national and foreign holders of qualifications to assist them in gaining professional recognition of their qualifications, and to employers who need advice on the professional recognition of foreign qualifications. Information should also be easily accessible to current and potential students;

(b) Establish and maintain contacts between the professional bodies of both sending and receiving countries, higher education institutions/providers, quality assurance and accreditation bodies, as well as academic recognition bodies to improve qualification assessment methodologies;

(c) Establish, develop and implement assessment criteria and procedures for comparing programmes and qualifications to facilitate the recognition of qualifications and to accommodate learning outcomes and competencies that are culturally appropriate in addition to input and process requirements;

(d) Improve the accessibility at the international level of upto-date, accurate and comprehensive information on mutual recognition agreements for the professions and encourage the development of new agreements.

9

WORLD DECLARATION ON HIGHER EDUCATION FOR TWENTY-FIRST CENTURY: VISION AND ACTION

(Adopted by the World Conference on Higher Education, Higher Education in the Twenty-First Century: Vision and Action, 9 October 1998)

PREAMBLE

On the eve of a new century, there is an unprecedented demand for and a great diversification in higher education, as well as an increased awareness of its vital importance for sociocultural and economic development, and for building the future, for which the younger generations will need to be equipped with new skills, knowledge and ideals. Higher education includes 'all types of studies, training or training for research at the post-secondary level, provided by universities or other educational establishments that are approved as institutions of higher education by the competent State authorities'. Everywhere higher education is faced with great challenges and difficulties related to financing, equity of conditions at access into and during the course of studies, improved staff development, skills-based training, enhancement and preservation of quality in teaching, research and services, relevance of programmes, employability of graduates, establishment of efficient co-operation agreements and equitable access to the benefits of international co-operation. At the same time, higher education is being challenged by new opportunities relating to technologies that are improving the ways in which knowledge can be produced, managed, disseminated, accessed and controlled. Equitable access to these technologies should be ensured at all levels of education systems.

The second half of this century will go down in the history of higher education as the period of its most spectacular expansion: an over sixfold increase in student enrolments worldwide, from 13 million in 1960 to 82 million in 1995. But it is also the period which has seen the gap between industrially developed, the developing countries and in particular the least developed countries with regard to access and resources for higher learning and research, already enormous, becoming even wider. It has also been a period of increased socio-economic stratification and greater difference in educational opportunity within countries, including in some of the most developed and wealthiest nations. Without adequate higher education and research institutions providing a critical mass of skilled and educated people, no country can ensure genuine endogenous and sustainable development and, in particular, developing countries and least developed countries cannot reduce the gap separating them from the industrially developed ones. Sharing knowledge, international co-operation and new technologies can offer new opportunities to reduce this gap.

Higher education has given ample proof of its viability over the centuries and of its ability to change and to induce change and progress in society. Owing to the scope and pace of change, society has become increasingly knowledge-based so that higher learning and research now act as essential components of cultural, socio-economic and environmentally sustainable development of individuals, communities and nations. Higher education itself is confronted therefore with formidable challenges and must proceed to the most radical change and renewal it has ever been required to undertake, so that our society, which is currently undergoing a profound crisis of values, can transcend mere economic considerations and incorporate deeper dimensions of morality and spirituality.

It is with the aim of providing solutions to these challenges and of setting in motion a process of in-depth reform in higher education worldwide that UNESCO has convened a World Conference on Higher Education in the Twenty-First Century: Vision and Action. In preparation for the Conference, UNESCO issued, in 1995, its Policy Paper for Change and Development in Higher Education. Five regional consultations (Havana, November 1996; Dakar, April 1997; Tokyo, July 1997; Palermo, September 1997; and Beirut, March 1998) were subsequently held. The Declarations and Plans of Action adopted by them, each preserving its own specificity, are duly taken into account in the present Declaration—as is the whole process of reflection undertaken by the preparation of the World Conference—and are annexed to it.

We, participants in the World Conference on Higher Education, assembled at UNESCO Headquarters in Paris, from 5 to 9 October 1998.

Recalling the principles of the Charter of the United Nations, the Universal Declaration of Human Rights, the International Covenant on Economic, Social and Cultural Rights, and the International Covenant on Civil and Political Rights.

Recalling also the Universal Declaration of Human Rights which states in Article 26, paragraph 1, that 'Everyone has the right to education' and that 'higher education shall be equally accessible to all on the basis of merit', and endorsing the basic principles of the Convention against Discrimination in Education (1960), which, by Article 4, commits the States Parties to it to 'make higher education equally accessible to all on the basis of individual capacity'.

Taking into account the recommendations concerning higher education of major commissions and conferences, inter alia, the International Commission on Education for the Twenty-First Century, the World Commission on Culture and Development, the 44th and 45th sessions of the International Conference on Education (Geneva, 1994 and 1996), the decisions taken at the 27th and 29th sessions of UNESCO's General Conference, in particular regarding the Recommendation concerning the Status of Higher-Education Teaching Personnel, the World Conference on Education for All (Jomtien, Thailand, 1990), the United Nations Conference on Environment and Development (Rio de Janeiro, 1992), the Conference on Academic Freedom and University Autonomy (Sinaia, 1992), the World Conference on Human Rights (Vienna, 1993), the World Summit for Social Development (Copenhagen, 1995), the fourth World Conference on Women (Beijing, 1995), the International Congress on Education and Informatics (Moscow, 1996), the World Congress on Higher Education and Human Resources Development for the Twenty-First Century (Manila, 1997), the fifth International Conference on Adult Education (Hamburg, 1997) and especially the Agenda for the Future under Theme 2 (Improving the conditions and quality of learning) stating: 'We commit ourselves to ... opening schools, colleges and universities to adult learners ... by calling upon the World Conference on Higher Education

(Paris, 1998) to promote the transformation of post-secondary institutions into lifelong learning institutions and to define the role of universities accordingly'.

Convinced that education is a fundamental pillar of human rights, democracy, sustainable development and peace, and shall therefore become accessible to all throughout life and that measures are required to ensure co-ordination and co-operation across and between the various sectors, particularly between general, technical and professional secondary and post-secondary education as well as between universities, colleges and technical institutions.

Believing that, in this context, the solution of the problems faced on the eve of the twenty-first century will be determined by the vision of the future society and by the role that is assigned to education in general and to higher education in particular.

Aware that on the threshold of a new millennium it is the duty of higher education to ensure that the values and ideals of a culture of peace prevail and that the intellectual community should be mobilised to that end.

Considering that a substantial change and development of higher education, the enhancement of its quality and relevance, and the solution to the major challenges it faces, require the strong involvement not only of governments and of higher education institutions, but also of all stakeholders, including students and their families, teachers, business and industry, the public and private sectors of the economy, parliaments, the media, the community, professional associations and society as well as a greater responsibility of higher education institutions towards society and accountability in the use of public and private, national or international resources.

Emphasising that higher education systems should enhance their capacity to live with uncertainty, to change and bring about change, and to address social needs and to promote solidarity and equity; should preserve and exercise scientific rigour and originality, in a spirit of impartiality, as a basic prerequisite for attaining and sustaining an indispensable level of quality; and should place students at the centre of their concerns, within a lifelong perspective, so as to allow their full integration into the global knowledge society of the coming century.

Also believing that international co-operation and exchange are major avenues for advancing higher education throughout the world, Proclaim the following:

MISSIONS AND FUNCTIONS OF HIGHER EDUCATION

Article 1. Mission to Educate, to Train and to undertake Research

We affirm that the core missions and values of higher education, in particular the mission to contribute to the sustainable development and improvement of society as a whole, should be preserved, reinforced and further expanded, namely, to:

(a) educate highly qualified graduates and responsible citizens able to meet the needs of all sectors of human activity, by offering relevant qualifications, including professional training, which combine high-level knowledge and skills, using courses and content continually tailored to the present and future needs of society;

(b) provide opportunities (espace ouvert) for higher learning and for learning throughout life, giving to learners an optimal range of choice and a flexibility of entry and exit points within the system, as well as an opportunity for individual development and social mobility in order to educate for citizenship and for active participation in society, with a worldwide vision, for endogenous capacity-building, and for the consolidation of human rights, sustainable development, democracy and peace, in a context of justice;

(c) advance, create and disseminate knowledge through research and provide, as part of its service to the community, relevant expertise to assist societies in cultural, social and economic development, promoting and developing scientific and technological research as well as research in the social sciences, the humanities and the creative arts;

(d) help understand, interpret, preserve, enhance, promote and disseminate national and regional, international and historic cultures, in a context of cultural pluralism and diversity;

(e) help protect and enhance societal values by training young people in the values which form the basis of democratic citizenship and by providing critical and detached perspectives to assist in the discussion of strategic options and the reinforcement of humanistic perspectives;

(f) contribute to the development and improvement of education at all levels, including through the training of teachers.

Article 2. Ethical Role, Autonomy, Responsibility and Anticipatory Function

In accordance with the Recommendation concerning the Status of Higher-Education Teaching Personnel approved by the General Conference of UNESCO in November 1997, higher education institutions and their personnel and students should:

(a) preserve and develop their crucial functions, through the exercise of ethics and scientific and intellectual rigour in their various activities;

(b) be able to speak out on ethical, cultural and social problems completely independently and in full awareness of their responsibilities, exercising a kind of intellectual authority that society needs to help it to reflect, understand and act;

(c) enhance their critical and forward-looking functions, through continuing analysis of emerging social, economic, cultural and political trends, providing a focus for forecasting, warning and prevention;

(d) exercise their intellectual capacity and their moral prestige to defend and actively disseminate universally accepted values, including peace, justice, freedom, equality and solidarity, as enshrined in UNESCO's Constitution;

(e) enjoy full academic autonomy and freedom, conceived as a set of rights and duties, while being fully responsible and accountable to society;

(f) play a role in helping identify and address issues that affect the well-being of communities, nations and global society.

SHAPING A NEW VISION OF HIGHER EDUCATION

Article 3. Equity of Access

(a) In keeping with Article 26.1 of the Universal Declaration of Human Rights, admission to higher education should be based on the merit, capacity, efforts, perseverance and devotion, showed by those seeking access to it, and can take place in a lifelong scheme, at any time, with due recognition of previously acquired skills. As a consequence, no discrimination can be accepted in granting access to higher education on grounds of race, gender, language or religion, or economic, cultural or social distinctions, or physical disabilities.

(b) Equity of access to higher education should begin with the reinforcement and, if need be, the reordering of its links with all other levels of education, particularly with secondary education. Higher education institutions must be viewed as, and must also work within themselves to be a part of and encourage, a seamless system starting with early childhood and primary education and continuing through life. Higher education institutions must work in active partnership with parents, schools, students, socio-economic groups and communities. Secondary education should not only prepare qualified candidates for access to higher education by developing the capacity to learn on a broad basis but also open the way to active life by providing training on a wide range of jobs. However, access to higher education should remain open to those successfully completing secondary school, or its equivalent, or presenting entry qualifications, as far as possible, at any age and without any discrimination.

(c) As a consequence, the rapid and wide-reaching demand for higher education requires, where appropriate, all policies concerning access to higher education to give priority in the future to the approach based on the merit of the individual, as defined in Article 3(a) above.

(d) Access to higher education for members of some special target groups, such as indigenous peoples, cultural and linguistic minorities, disadvantaged groups, peoples living under occupation and those who suffer from disabilities, must be actively facilitated, since these groups as collectivities and as individuals may have both experience and talent that can be of great value for the development of societies and nations. Special material help and educational solutions can help overcome the obstacles that these groups face, both in accessing and in continuing higher education.

Article 4. Enhancing Participation and Promoting the Role of Women

(a) Although significant progress has been achieved to enhance the access of women to higher education, various socio-economic, cultural and political obstacles continue in many places in the world to impede their full access and effective integration. To overcome them remains an urgent priority in the renewal process for ensuring an equitable and nondiscriminatory system of higher education based on the principle of merit.

(b) Further efforts are required to eliminate all gender stereotyping in higher education, to consider gender aspects in different disciplines and to consolidate women's participation at all levels and in all disciplines, in which they are under-represented and, in particular, to enhance their active involvement in decision-making.

(c) Gender studies (women's studies) should be promoted as a field of knowledge, strategic for the transformation of higher education and society.

(d) Efforts should be made to eliminate political and social barriers whereby women are under-represented and in particular to enhance their active involvement at policy and decisionmaking levels within higher education and society.

Article 5. Advancing Knowledge through Research in Science, Arts and Humanities and the Dissemination of its Results

(a) The advancement of knowledge through research is an essential function of all systems of higher education, which should promote postgraduate studies. Innovation, interdisciplinarity and transdisciplinarity should be promoted and reinforced in programmes with long-term orientations on social and cultural aims and needs. An appropriate balance should be established between basic and target-oriented research.

(b) Institutions should ensure that all members of the academic community engaged in research are provided with appropriate training, resources and support. The intellectual and cultural rights on the results of research should be used to the benefit of humanity and should be protected so that they cannot be abused.

(c) Research must be enhanced in all disciplines, including the social and human sciences, education (including higher education), engineering, natural sciences, mathematics, informatics and the arts within the framework of national, regional and international research and development policies. Of special importance is the enhancement of research capacities in higher education research institutions, as mutual enhancement of quality takes place when higher education and research are conducted at a high level within the same institution. These institutions should find the material and financial support required, from both public and private sources.

Article 6. Long-term Orientation Based on Relevance

(a) Relevance in higher education should be assessed in terms of the fit between what society expects of institutions and what they do. This requires ethical standards, political impartiality, critical capacities and, at the same time, a better articulation with the problems of society and the world of work, basing long-term orientations on societal aims and needs, including respect for cultures and environmental protection. The concern is to provide access to both broad general education and targeted, career-specific education, often interdisciplinary, focusing on skills and aptitudes, both of which equip individuals to live in a variety of changing settings, and to be able to change occupations.

(b) Higher education should reinforce its role of service to society, especially its activities aimed at eliminating poverty, intolerance, violence, illiteracy, hunger, environmental degradation and disease, mainly through an interdisciplinary and transdisciplinary approach in the analysis of problems and issues.

(c) Higher education should enhance its contribution to the development of the whole education system, notably through improved teacher education, curriculum development and educational research.

(d) Ultimately, higher education should aim at the creation of a new society—non-violent and non-exploitative—consisting of highly cultivated, motivated and integrated individuals, inspired by love for humanity and guided by wisdom.

Article 7. Strengthening Co-operation with the World of Work and Analysing and Anticipating Societal Needs

(a) In economies characterised by changes and the emergence of new production paradigms based on knowledge and its application, and on the handling of information, the links between higher education, the world of work and other parts of society should be strengthened and renewed.

(b) Links with the world of work can be strengthened, through the participation of its representatives in the governance of institutions, the increased use of domestic and international apprenticeship/work-study opportunities for students and teachers, the exchange of personnel between the world of work and higher education institutions and revised curricula more closely aligned with working practices.

(c) As a lifelong source of professional training, updating and recycling, institutions of higher education should systematically take into account trends in the world of work and in the scientific, technological and economic sectors. In order to respond to the work requirements, higher education systems and the world of work should jointly develop and assess learning processes, bridging programmes and prior learning assessment and recognition programmes, which integrate theory and training on the job. Within the framework of their anticipatory function, higher education institutions could contribute to the creation of new jobs, although that is not their only function.

(d) Developing entrepreneurial skills and initiative should become major concerns of higher education, in order to facilitate employability of graduates who will increasingly be called upon to be not only job seekers but also and above all to become job creators. Higher education institutions should give the opportunity to students to fully develop their own abilities with a sense of social responsibility, educating them to become full participants in democratic society and promoters of changes that will foster equity and justice.

Article 8. Diversification for Enhanced Equity of Opportunity

(a) Diversifying higher education models and recruitment methods and criteria is essential both to meet increasing international demand and to provide access to various delivery modes and to extend access to an ever-wider public, in a lifelong perspective, based on flexible entry and exit points to and from the system of higher education.

(b) More diversified systems of higher education are characterised by new types of tertiary institutions: public, private and non-profit institutions, amongst others. Institutions should be able to offer a wide variety of education and training opportunities: traditional degrees, short courses, part-time study, flexible schedules, modularised courses, supported learning at a distance, etc.

Article 9. Innovative Educational Approaches: Critical Thinking and Creativity

(a) In a world undergoing rapid changes, there is a perceived need for a new vision and paradigm of higher education, which should be student-oriented, calling in most countries for in-depth reforms and an open access policy so as to cater for ever more diversified categories of people, and of its contents, methods, practices and means of delivery, based on new types of links and partnerships with the community and with the broadest sectors of society.

(b) Higher education institutions should educate students to become well informed and deeply motivated citizens, who can think critically, analyse problems of society, look for solutions to the problems of society, apply them and accept social responsibilities.

(c) To achieve these goals, it may be necessary to recast curricula, using new and appropriate methods, so as to go beyond cognitive mastery of disciplines. New pedagogical and didactical approaches should be accessible and promoted in order to facilitate the acquisition of skills, competences and abilities for communication, creative and critical analysis, independent thinking and team work in multicultural contexts, where creativity also involves combining traditional or local knowledge and know-how with advanced science and technology. These recast curricula should take into account the gender dimension and the specific cultural, historic and economic context of each country. The teaching of human rights standards and education on the needs of communities in all parts of the world should be reflected in the curricula of all disciplines, particularly those preparing for entrepreneurship. Academic personnel should play a significant role in determining the curriculum.

(d) New methods of education will also imply new types of teaching-learning materials. These have to be coupled with new methods of testing that will promote not only powers of memory but also powers of comprehension, skills for practical work and creativity.

Article 10. Higher Education Personnel and Students as Major Actors

(a) A vigorous policy of staff development is an essential element for higher education institutions. Clear policies should be established concerning higher education teachers, who nowadays need to focus on teaching students how to learn and how to take initiatives rather than being exclusively founts of knowledge. Adequate provision should be made for research and for updating and improving pedagogical skills, through appropriate staff development programmes, encouraging constant innovation in curriculum, teaching and learning methods, and ensuring appropriate professional and financial status, and for excellence in research and teaching, reflecting the corresponding provisions of the Recommendation concerning the Status of Higher-Education Teaching Personnel approved by the General Conference of UNESCO in November 1997. To this end, more importance should be attached to international experience. Furthermore, in view of the role of higher education for lifelong learning, experience outside the institutions ought to be considered as a relevant qualification for higher educational staff.

(b) Clear policies should be established by all higher education institutions preparing teachers of early childhood education and for primary and secondary schools, providing stimulus for constant innovation in curriculum, best practices in teaching methods and familiarity with diverse learning styles. It is vital to have appropriately trained administrative and technical personnel.

(c) National and institutional decision-makers should place students and their needs at the centre of their concerns, and should consider them as major partners and responsible stakeholders in the renewal of higher education. This should include student involvement in issues that affect that level of education, in evaluation, the renovation of teaching methods and curricula and, in the institutional framework in force, in policy-formulation and institutional management. As students have the right to organise and represent themselves, students' involvement in these issues should be guaranteed.

(d) Guidance and counselling services should be developed, in co-operation with student organisations, in order to assist students in the transition to higher education at whatever age and to take account of the needs of ever more diversified categories of learners. Apart from those entering higher education from schools or further education colleges, they should also take account of the needs of those leaving and returning in a lifelong process. Such support is important in ensuring a good match between student and course, reducing dropout. Students who do drop out should have suitable opportunities to return to higher education if and when appropriate.

FROM VISION TO ACTION

Article 11. Qualitative Evaluation

(a) Quality in higher education is a multidimensional concept, which should embrace all its functions, and activities: teaching and academic programmes, research and scholarship, staffing, students, buildings, facilities, equipment, services to the community and the academic environment. Internal self-evaluation and external review, conducted openly by independent specialists, if possible with international expertise, are vital for enhancing quality. Independent national bodies should be established and comparative standards of quality, recognised at international level, should be defined. Due attention should be paid to specific institutional, national and regional contexts in order to take into account diversity and to avoid uniformity. Stakeholders should be an integral part of the institutional evaluation process.

(b) Quality also requires that higher education should be characterised by its international dimension: exchange of knowledge, interactive networking, mobility of teachers and students, and international research projects, while taking into account the national cultural values and circumstances.

(c) To attain and sustain national, regional or international quality, certain components are particularly relevant, notably careful selection of staff and continuous staff development, in particular through the promotion of appropriate programmes for academic staff development, including teaching/learning methodology and mobility between countries, between higher education institutions, and between higher education institutions and the world of work, as well as student mobility within and between countries. The new information technologies are an important tool in this process, owing to their impact on the acquisition of knowledge and know-how.

Article 12. The Potential and the Challenge of Technology

The rapid breakthroughs in new information and communication technologies will further change the way knowledge is developed, acquired and delivered. It is also important to note that the new technologies offer opportunities to innovate on course content and teaching methods and to widen access to higher learning. However, it should be borne in mind that new information technology does not reduce the need for teachers but changes their role in relation to the learning process and that the continuous dialogue that converts information into knowledge and understanding becomes fundamental. Higher education institutions should lead in drawing on the advantages and potential of new information and communication technologies, ensuring quality and maintaining high standards for education practices and outcomes in a spirit of openness, equity and international cooperation by:

(a) engaging in networks, technology transfer, capacity-building, developing teaching materials and sharing experience of their application in teaching, training and research, making knowledge accessible to all;

(b) creating new learning environments, ranging from distance education facilities to complete virtual higher education institutions and systems, capable of bridging distances and developing high-quality systems of education, thus serving social and economic advancement and democratisation as well as other relevant priorities of society, while ensuring that these virtual education facilities, based on regional, continental or global networks, function in a way that respects cultural and social identities;

(c) noting that, in making full use of information and communication technology (ICT) for educational purposes, particular attention should be paid to removing the grave inequalities which exist among and also within the countries of the world with regard to access to new information and communication technologies and to the production of the corresponding resources;

(d) adapting ICT to national, regional and local needs and securing technical, educational, management and institutional systems to sustain it;

(e) facilitating, through international co-operation, the identification of the objectives and interests of all countries, particularly the developing countries, equitable access and the strengthening of infrastructures in this field and the dissemination of such technology throughout society;

(f) closely following the evolution of the 'knowledge society' in order to ensure high quality and equitable regulations for access to prevail;

(g) taking the new possibilities created by the use of ICTs into account, while realising that it is, above all, institutions of higher education that are using ICTs in order to modernise their work, and not ICTs transforming institutions of higher education from real to virtual institutions.

Article 13. Strengthening Higher Education Management and Financing

(a) The management and financing of higher education require the development of appropriate planning and policy-analysis capacities and strategies, based on partnerships established between higher education institutions and state and national planning and co-ordination bodies, so as to secure appropriately streamlined management and the cost-effective use of resources. Higher education institutions should adopt forwardlooking management practices that respond to the needs of their environments. Managers in higher education must be responsive, competent and able to evaluate regularly, by internal and external mechanisms, the effectiveness of procedures and administrative rules.

(b) Higher education institutions must be given autonomy to manage their internal affairs, but with this autonomy must come clear and transparent accountability to the government, parliament, students and the wider society.

(c) The ultimate goal of management should be to enhance the institutional mission by ensuring high-quality teaching, training and research, and services to the community. This objective requires governance that combines social vision, including understanding of global issues, with efficient managerial skills. Leadership in higher education is thus a major social responsibility and can be significantly strengthened through dialogue with all stakeholders, especially teachers and students, in higher education. The participation of teaching faculty in the governing bodies of higher education institutions should be taken into account, within the framework of current institutional arrangements, bearing in mind the need to keep the size of these bodies within reasonable bounds.

(d) The promotion of North-South co-operation to ensure the necessary financing for strengthening higher education in the developing countries is essential.

Article 14. Financing of Higher Education as a Public Service

The funding of higher education requires both public and private resources. The role of the state remains essential in this regard.

(a) The diversification of funding sources reflects the support that society provides to higher education and must be further strengthened to ensure the development of higher education, increase its efficiency and maintain its quality and relevance. Public support for higher education and research remains essential to ensure a balanced achievement of educational and social missions.

(b) Society as a whole must support education at all levels, including higher education, given its role in promoting sustainable economic, social and cultural development. Mobilisation for this purpose depends on public awareness and involvement of the public and private sectors of the economy, parliaments, the media, governmental and non-governmental organisations, students as well as institutions, families and all the social actors involved with higher education.

Article 15. Sharing Knowledge and Know-how across Borders and Continents

(a) The principle of solidarity and true partnership amongst higher education institutions worldwide is crucial for education and training in all fields that encourage an understanding of global issues, the role of democratic governance and skilled human resources in their resolution, and the need for living together with different cultures and values. The practice of multilingualism, faculty and student exchange programmes and institutional linkage to promote intellectual and scientific co-operation should be an integral part of all higher education systems.

(b) The principles of international co-operation based on solidarity, recognition and mutual support, true partnership that equitably serves the interests of the partners and the value of sharing knowledge and know-how across borders should govern relationships among higher education institutions in both developed and developing countries and should benefit the least developed countries in particular. Consideration should be given to the need for safeguarding higher education institutional capacities in regions suffering from conflict or natural disasters. Consequently, an international dimension should permeate the curriculum, and the teaching and learning processes.

(c) Regional and international normative instruments for the recognition of studies should be ratified and implemented, including certification of the skills, competences and abilities of graduates, making it easier for students to change courses, in order to facilitate mobility within and between national systems.

Article 16—From 'Brain Drain' to 'Brain Gain'

The 'brain drain' has yet to be stemmed, since it continues to deprive the developing countries and those in transition, of the high-level expertise necessary to accelerate their socio-economic progress. International co-operation schemes should be based on long-term partnerships between institutions in the South and the North, and also promote South-South co-operation.

Priority should be given to training programmes in the developing countries, in centres of excellence forming regional and international networks, with short periods of specialised and intensive study abroad. Consideration should be given to creating an environment conducive to attracting and retaining skilled human capital, either through national policies or international arrangements to facilitate the return—permanent or temporary—of highly trained scholars and researchers to their countries of origin. At the same time, efforts must be directed towards a process of 'brain gain' through collaboration programmes that, by virtue of their international dimension, enhance the building and strengthening of institutions and facilitate full use of endogenous capacities. Experience gained through the UNITWIN/UNESCO Chairs Programme and the principles enshrined in the regional conventions on the recognition of degrees and diplomas in higher education are of particular importance in this respect.

Article 17. Partnership and Alliances

Partnership and alliances amongst stakeholders—national and institutional policy-makers, teaching and related staff, researchers and students, and administrative and technical personnel in institutions of higher education, the world of work, community groups—is a powerful force in managing change. Also, non-governmental organisations are key actors in this process. Henceforth, partnership, based on common interest, mutual respect and credibility, should be a prime matrix for renewal in higher education.

We, the participants in the World Conference on Higher Education, adopt this Declaration and reaffirm the right of all people to education and the right of access to higher education based on individual merit and capacity;

We pledge to act together within the frame of our individual and collective responsibilities, by taking all necessary measures in order to realise the principles concerning higher education contained in the Universal Declaration of Human Rights and in the Convention against Discrimination in Education;

We solemnly reaffirm our commitment to peace. To that end, we are determined to accord high priority to education for peace and to participate in the celebration of the International Year for the Culture of Peace in the year 2000;

We adopt, therefore, this World Declaration on Higher Education for the Twenty-First Century: Vision and Action. To achieve the goals set forth in this Declaration and, in particular, for immediate action, we agree on the following Framework for Priority Action for Change and Development of Higher Education.

FRAMEWORK FOR PRIORITY ACTION FOR CHANGE AND DEVELOPMENT OF HIGHER EDUCATION

I. Priority Actions At National Level

1. States, including their governments, parliaments and other decision-makers, should:
   (a) establish, where appropriate, the legislative, political and financial framework for the reform and further development of higher education, in keeping with the terms of the Universal Declaration of Human Rights, which establishes that higher education shall be 'accessible to all on the basis of merit'. No discrimination can be accepted, no one can be excluded from higher education or its study fields, degree levels and types of institutions on grounds of race, gender, language, religion, or age or because of any

economic or social distinctions or physical disabilities;

(b) reinforce the links between higher education and research;

(c) consider and use higher education as a catalyst for the entire education system;

(d) develop higher education institutions to include lifelong learning approaches, giving learners an optimal range of choice and a flexibility of entry and exit points within the system, and redefine their role accordingly, which implies the development of open and continuous access to higher learning and the need for bridging programmes and prior learning assessment and recognition;

(e) make efforts, when necessary, to establish close links between higher education and research institutions, taking into account the fact that education and research are two closely related elements in the establishment of knowledge;

(f) develop innovative schemes of collaboration between institutions of higher education and different sectors of society to ensure that higher education and research programmes effectively contribute to local, regional and national development;

(g) fulfil their commitments to higher education and be accountable for the pledges adopted with their concurrence, at several forums, particularly over the past decade, with regard to human, material and financial resources, human development and education in general, and to higher education in particular;

(h) have a policy framework to ensure new partnerships and the involvement of all relevant stakeholders in all aspects of higher education: the evaluation process, including curriculum and pedagogical renewal, and guidance and counselling services; and, in the framework of existing institutional arrangements, policy-making and institutional governance;

(i) define and implement policies to eliminate all gender stereotyping in higher education and to consolidate women's participation at all levels and in all disciplines in which they are under-represented at present and, in particular, to enhance their active involvement in decision-making;

(j) establish clear policies concerning higher education teachers, as set out in the Recommendation concerning the Status of Higher-Education Teaching Personnel approved by the General Conference of UNESCO in November 1997;

(k) recognise students as the centre of attention of higher education, and one of its stakeholders. They should be involved, by means of adequate institutional structures, in the renewal of their level of education (including curriculum and pedagogical reform), and policy decision, in the framework of existing institutional arrangements;

(l) recognise that students have the right to organise themselves autonomously;

(m) promote and facilitate national and international mobility of teaching staff and students as an essential part of the quality and relevance of higher education;

(n) provide and ensure those conditions necessary for the exercise of academic freedom and institutional autonomy so as to allow institutions of higher education, as well as those individuals engaged in higher education and research, to fulfil their obligations to society.

2. States in which enrolment in higher education is low by internationally accepted comparative standards should strive to ensure a level of higher education adequate for relevant needs in the public and private sectors of society and to establish plans for diversifying and expanding access, particularly benefiting all minorities and disadvantaged groups.

3. The interface with general, technical and professional secondary education should be reviewed in depth, in the context of lifelong learning. Access to higher education in whatever form must remain open to those successfully completing secondary education or its equivalent or meeting entry qualifications at any age, while creating gateways to higher education, especially for older students without any formal secondary education certificates, by attaching more importance to their professional experience.

   However, preparation for higher education should not be the sole or primary purpose of secondary education, which should also prepare for the world of work, with complementary training whenever required, in order to provide knowledge, capacities and skills for a wide range of jobs. The concept of bridging programmes should be promoted to allow those entering the job market to return to studies at a later date.

4. Concrete steps should be taken to reduce the widening gap between industrially developed and developing countries, in particular the least developed countries, with regard to higher

education and research. Concrete steps are also needed to encourage increased co-operation between countries at all levels of economic development with regard to higher education and research. Consideration should be given to making budgetary provisions for that purpose, and developing mutually beneficial agreements involving industry, national as well as international, in order to sustain co-operative activities and projects through appropriate incentives and funding in education, research and the development of high-level experts in these countries.

II. Priority Actions at the Level of Systems and Institutions

5. Each higher education institution should define its mission according to the present and future needs of society and base it on an awareness of the fact that higher education is essential for any country or region to reach the necessary level of sustainable and environmentally sound economic and social development, cultural creativity nourished by better knowledge and understanding of the cultural heritage, higher living standards, and internal and international harmony and peace, based on human rights, democracy, tolerance and mutual respect. These missions should incorporate the concept of academic freedom set out in the Recommendation concerning the Status of Higher-Education Teaching Personnel approved by the General Conference of UNESCO in November 1997.

6. In establishing priorities in their programmes and structures, higher education institutions should:

(a) take into account the need to abide by the rules of ethics and scientific and intellectual rigour, and the multidisciplinary and transdisciplinary approach;

(b) be primarily concerned to establish systems of access for the benefit of all persons who have the necessary abilities and motivations;

(c) use their autonomy and high academic standards to contribute to the sustainable development of society and to the resolution of the issues facing the society of the future. They should develop their capacity to give forewarning through the analysis of emerging social, cultural, economic and political trends, approached in a multidisciplinary and transdisciplinary manner, giving particular attention to:

— high quality, a clear sense of the social pertinence of studies and their anticipatory function, based on scientific grounds;

— knowledge of fundamental social questions, in particular related to the elimination of poverty, to sustainable development, to intercultural dialogue and to the shaping of a culture of peace;

— the need for close connection with effective research organisations or institutions that perform well in the sphere of research;

— the development of the whole education system in the perspective of the recommendations and the new goals for education as set out in the 1996 report to UNESCO of the International Commission on Education for the Twenty-first Century;

– fundamentals of human ethics, applied to each profession and to all areas of human endeavour;

(d) ensure, especially in universities and as far as possible, that faculty members participate in teaching, research, tutoring students and steering institutional affairs;

(e) take all necessary measures to reinforce their service to the community, especially their activities aimed at eliminating poverty, intolerance, violence, illiteracy, hunger and disease, through an interdisciplinary and transdisciplinary approach in the analysis of challenges, problems and different subjects;

(f) set their relations with the world of work on a new basis involving effective partnerships with all social actors concerned, starting from a reciprocal harmonisation of action and the search for solutions to pressing problems of humanity, all this within a framework of responsible autonomy and academic freedoms;

(g) ensure high quality of international standing, consider accountability and both internal and external evaluation, with due respect for autonomy and academic freedom, as being normal and inherent in their functioning, and institutionalise transparent systems, structures or mechanisms specific thereto;

(h) as lifelong education requires academic staff to update and improve their teaching skills and learning methods, even more than in the present systems mainly based on short periods of higher teaching, establish appropriate academic staff development structures and/or mechanisms and programmes;

(i) promote and develop research, which is a necessary feature of all higher education systems, in all disciplines, including the human and social sciences and arts, given their relevance for development. Also, research on higher education itself should be strengthened through mechanisms such as the UNESCO/UNU Forum on Higher Education and the UNESCO Chairs in Higher Education. Objective, timely studies are needed to ensure continued progress towards such key national objectives as access, equity, quality, relevance and diversification;

(j) remove gender inequalities and biases in curricula and research, and take all appropriate measures to ensure balanced representation of both men and women among students and teachers, at all levels of management;

(k) provide, where appropriate, guidance and counselling, remedial courses, training in how to study and other forms of student support, including measures to improve student living conditions.

7. While the need for closer links between higher education and the world of work is important worldwide, it is particularly vital for the developing countries and especially the least developed countries, given their low level of economic development. Governments of these countries should take appropriate measures to reach this objective through appropriate measures such as strengthening institutions for higher/professional/vocational education. At the same time, international action is needed in order to help establish joint undertakings between higher education and industry in these countries. It will be

necessary to give consideration to ways in which higher education graduates could be supported, through various schemes, following the positive experience of the micro-credit system and other incentives, in order to start small- and medium-size enterprises. At the institutional level, developing entrepreneurial skills and initiative should become a major concern of higher education, in order to facilitate employability of graduates who will increasingly be required not only to be job-seekers but to become job-creators.

8. The use of new technologies should be generalised to the greatest extent possible to help higher education institutions, to reinforce academic development, to widen access, to attain universal scope and to extend knowledge, as well as to facilitate education throughout life. Governments, educational institutions and the private sector should ensure that informatics and communication network infrastructures, computer facilities and human resources training are adequately provided.

9. Institutions of higher education should be open to adult learners:

   (a) by developing coherent mechanisms to recognise the outcomes of learning undertaken in different contexts, and to ensure that credit is transferable within and between institutions, sectors and states;

   (b) by establishing joint higher education/ community research and training partnerships, and by bringing the services of higher education institutions to outside groups;

   (c) by carrying out interdisciplinary research in all aspects of adult education and learning with the participation of adult learners themselves;

(d) by creating opportunities for adult learning in flexible, open and creative ways.

III. ACTIONS TO BE TAKEN AT INTERNATIONAL LEVEL AND, IN PARTICULAR, TO BE INITIATED BY UNESCO

10. Co-operation should be conceived of as an integral part of the institutional missions of higher education institutions and systems. Intergovernmental organisations, donor agencies and non-governmental organisations should extend their action in order to develop inter-university co-operation projects in particular through twinning institutions, based on solidarity and partnership, as a means of bridging the gap between rich and poor countries in the vital areas of knowledge production and application. Each institution of higher education should envisage the creation of an appropriate structure and/or mechanism for promoting and managing international co-operation.

11. UNESCO, and other intergovernmental organisations and non-governmental organisations active in higher education, the states through their bilateral and multilateral co-operation programmes, the academic community and all concerned partners in society should further promote international academic mobility as a means to advance knowledge and knowledge-sharing in order to bring about and promote solidarity as a main element of the global knowledge society of tomorrow, including through strong support for the joint work plan (1999-2005) of the six intergovernmental committees in charge of the application of the regional conventions on the recognition of studies, degrees and diplomas in

higher education and through large-scale co-operative action involving, inter alia, the establishment of an educational credit transfer scheme, with particular emphasis on South-South co-operation, the needs of the least developed countries and of the small states with few higher education institutions or none at all.

12. Institutions of higher education in industrialised countries should strive to make arrangements for international co-operation with sister institutions in developing countries and in particular with those of poor countries. In their co-operation, the institutions should make efforts to ensure fair and just recognition of studies abroad. UNESCO should take initiatives to develop higher education throughout the world, setting itself clear-cut goals that could lead to tangible results. One method might be to implement projects in different regions renewing efforts towards creating and/or strengthening centres of excellence in developing countries, in particular through the UNITWIN/ UNESCO Chairs Programme, relying on networks of national, regional and international higher education institutions.

13. UNESCO, together with all concerned parts of society, should also undertake action in order to alleviate the negative effects of 'brain drain' and to shift to a dynamic process of 'brain gain'. An overall analysis is required in all regions of the world of the causes and effects of brain drain. A vigorous campaign should be launched through the concerted effort of the international community and on the basis of academic solidarity and should encourage the return to their home country of expatriate academics, as well as the involvement of university volunteers—newly retired academics or

young academics at the beginning of their career—who wish to teach and undertake research at higher education institutions in developing countries. At the same time it is essential to support the developing countries in their efforts to build and strengthen their own educational capacities.

14. Within this framework, UNESCO should:

(a) promote better co-ordination among inter-governmental, supranational and nongovernmental organisations, agencies and foundations that sponsor existing programmes and projects for international co-operation in higher education.

Furthermore, co-ordination efforts should take place in the context of national priorities. This could be conducive to the pooling and sharing of resources, avoid overlapping and promote better identification of projects, greater impact of action and increased assurance of their validity through collective agreement and review. Programmes aiming at the rapid transfer of knowledge, supporting institutional development and establishing centres of excellence in all areas of knowledge, in particular for peace education, conflict resolution, human rights and democracy, should be supported by institutions and by public and private donors;

(b) jointly with the United Nations University and with National Commissions and various intergovernmental and non-governmental organisations, become a forum of reflection on higher education issues aiming at: (i) preparing update reports on the state of knowledge on higher education issues in all parts of the world; (ii) promoting innovative projects of training and research, intended to enhance the specific role of higher education in lifelong education; (iii) reinforcing international co-operation and emphasising the role of higher education for citizenship education, sustainable development and peace; and (iv) facilitating exchange of information and establishing, when appropriate, a database on successful experiences and innovations that can be consulted by institutions confronted with problems in their reforms of higher education;

(c) take specific action to support institutions of higher education in the least developed parts of the world and in regions suffering the effects of conflict or natural disasters;

(d) make renewed efforts towards creating or/and strengthening centres of excellence in developing countries;

(e) take the initiative to draw up an international instrument on academic freedom, autonomy and social responsibility in connection with the Recommendation concerning the Status of Higher-Education Teaching Personnel;

(f) ensure follow-up to the World Declaration on Higher Education and the Framework for Priority Action, jointly with other intergovernmental and non-governmental organisations and with all higher education stakeholders, including the United Nations University, the NGO Collective Consultation on Higher Education and the UNESCO Student Forum. It should have a crucial role in promoting international co-operation in the field of higher education in implementing this follow-up. Consideration should be given to according priority to this in the development of UNESCO's next draft Programme and Budget.

SUGGESTED READINGS

Barrow, Clyde, "The New Economy and Restructuring Higher Education," *Thought and Action*, Vol. XVI, Number 2, Fall 2000.

Bok, Derek, *Universities in the Marketplace: The Commercialization of Higher Education*, NJ: Princeton University Press, 2003.

Carr, Sarah, "A Day in the Life of a New Type of Professor," *The Chronicle of Higher Education*, 15 December 2000.

Coopers and Lybrand Learning Partnership Roundtable, *The Transformation of Higher Education in the Digital Age*, July 1997.

Hannah, Donald E., and associates, *Higher education in an era of digital competition : choices and challenges*, Madison, WI: Atwood Pub.,2000

Harasim, Linda M. and Starr Roxanne Hiltz, Lucio Teles, Murray Turoff, *Learning Networks : A Field Guide to Teaching and Learning Online*, 1995

Harry, Keith, ed., *Higher education through open and distance learning* , New York: Routledge, 1999

Hawisher, Gail E., Cynthia L. Selfe, *Evolving Perspectives on Computers and Composition Studies*, Urbana: NCTE. 1991

Katz, Richard N., "Dancing With the Devil : Information Technology and the New Competition in Higher Education" *Jossey-Bass Higher and AdultEducation Series*, Jossey-Bass Publishers, 1999.

Oblinger, Diana G. and Anne-Lee Verville, *What Business Wants From Higher Education*, Phoenix: The Oryx Press, 1998.

Porter, Lynnette R., *Creating the Virtual Classroom: Distance Learning with the Internet*, John Wiley & Sons, 1997.

Rowley, Daniel James and Lujan Herman, Herman D. Lujan, et al., *Strategic Choices for the Academy : How Demand for Lifelong Learning Will Re-Create Higher Education*, Jossey-Bass Publishers, 1998.

Shoemaker, Cynthia C. Jones, *Leadership in Continuing and Distance Education in Higher Education*, Allyn & Bacon, 1998.

Shumar, Wesley, *College for Sale: A Critique of the Commodification of Higher Education*, Washington, DC: The Falmer Press, 1997.

INDEX

objectives as access, eq